The Educative Community

THE PROFESSIONAL EDUCATION SERIES

Walter K. Beggs, *Editor*
Dean Emeritus, Teachers College, and
Professor of Educational Administration
University of Nebraska

Royce H. Knapp, *Research Editor*
Regents Professor of Education
University of Nebraska

The Educative Community

Linking the Community, School, and Family

by

ROGER HIEMSTRA

Assistant Professor of Education
University of Nebraska

PROFESSIONAL EDUCATORS PUBLICATIONS, INC.
LINCOLN, NEBRASKA

Library of Congress Catalog Card No.: 72-77986

ISBN   0-88224-006-4

Contents

5

CHAPTER 1

The Nature of the Community

WHAT IS A COMMUNITY?

What is a community? That is an interesting question to ask and a difficult one to answer. The difficulty lies in that many scholars have attempted to define community or to describe what makes up a community. The reader is referred to the various sources at the end of this chapter for a comprehensive study of the varied and contrasting conceptions of community.

The word "community" comes from the Latin word *Communis*, meaning fellowship or common relations and feelings. In its medieval usage the word was perhaps more descriptive, meaning a body of fellows or fellow townsmen. This definition is useful yet today, since the average person will probably define community as his home town, place of residence, or neighborhood.

There are many ways of examining the meaning of community beyond a locality reference. This does not mean that the community as a locality base is dying out; rather, the nature of the community is complex and changing. Thus, we need to be more precise if we are to understand the meaning of community well enough for effective living and survival in a situation of change.

One of the least precise ways of describing the community is to place it at either of two opposite poles. These polarities have been variously described as the range from rural to urban, from folk culture to mass culture, from simple organization to complex, and from Gemeinschaft to Gesellschaft (see the definitions at the end of the chapter). In whatever way these contrasting positions are described, they provide little assistance in helping one to describe the community he perceives.

On a slightly higher scale of precision, we can describe a community strictly on the basis of locality. This is perhaps the one community descriptor with which you are most familiar. Included would be such statements as: "Vicksburg, Michigan, is my home community!" "Watts is a black community!" "I live in the southeast part of Lincoln." Thus, you see that locality can range from a neighborhood to a small city to even a state. The difficulty in utilizing locality as a common reference base is this variability in size and area of inclusion as perceived by different people. However, the concept of locality will be utilized often in the remainder of this book when talking generally about communities.

A third manner in which we can think of community, and one precise enough to allow for some common understanding, is by looking at both the horizontal and vertical axes of a locality. This framework developed by Roland Warren is somewhat abstract, but it allows for the shared interests and patterns of behavior of people in one locality to be analyzed. We will utilize the framework to provide a basic definition for community. Figures 1 and 2 display the horizontal and vertical relationships.

The horizontal axis of the framework emphasizes the locality feature we described above. Think of it as people-to-people associations throughout a neighborhood or community. It involves the relationship of one individual to another individual or one group to another group in the same locality. An illustration would be a group of citizens coming together to form a public school curriculum council or the local United Fund organization sponsoring and administering the annual fund campaign. The organizing and coordinating roles performed are primarily local.

The framework's vertical axis emphasizes a feature of community activity that we have not yet mentioned, that of an individual's or a group's special interests. Here we are concerned with an individual's relationship to, or membership affiliation with, a local interest group that might in turn be associated with a state, regional, or national group. The person-to-person or person-to-group association is rooted in a locality base and branches upward into other and different locality bases. This can be illustrated by a teacher's membership in the local educational association which is on the horizontal axis and the relationship of this association with the National Educational Association on a vertical axis. The aim in either horizontal or vertical groups is to achieve some specific goal or resolve a particular problem.

The horizontal-vertical axes approach does not cover all aspects of "community" relationships. However, it does provide a basis for comparing Jane Smith, teacher, who lives on Woodward Avenue in Detroit to George Bailey, banker, who lives on Greenbriar Drive in Denver.

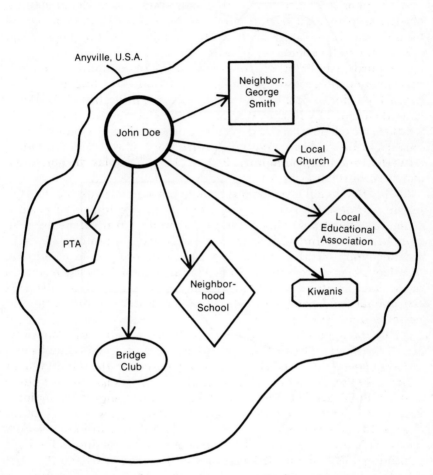

Figure 1. Community Horizontal Relationships

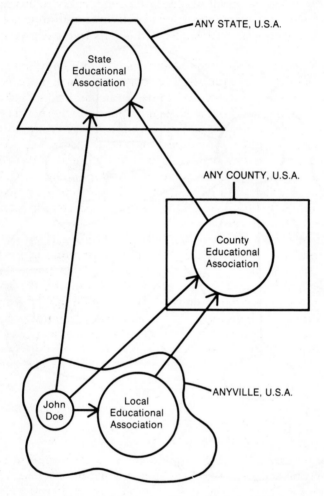

Figure 2. Community Vertical Relationships

For our purposes and to provide a common basis for comparison of people and groups, the following definition of community is offered: A community is "that combination of social units and systems which perform the major social functions having locality relevance."[1] In other words, the organization of social activities and units are designed in such a manner so as to facilitate the daily living of given sets of people.

The dynamic state of modern society, due to technology and many other factors, is leading to a progressive reorganization of daily living. The vertical relationships described above are becoming increasingly more important. One may hold a value judgment on whether this development is good or bad, but a shift from locality grouping toward interest grouping, or from horizontal grouping to vertical grouping, has been occurring for some years. Such shifting involves the entire workings of a community as a system of interdependent parts. Our definition should help put a handle on those relevant relationships and associations with which we will need to deal in later chapters on the role of education in communities.

It should be mentioned here that we have not discussed several of the diverse and contrasting definitions or conceptions of community. One may be interested in pursuing further the different notions of community such as the physical community, the social community, the economic community, the rural community, the urban community, the moral community, or the human community. Some scholars would rather study the community as space, as people, as shared activities, as relationships between people, as social processes, or as political activity. Several sources covering these approaches are suggested at the conclusion of this chapter.

THE CHANGING COMMUNITY

Developing and providing a rationale for a definition of community is complicated because of the dynamic nature of society. The increasing complexity of society and the rapidity of change is a reality sensed by most of us. Writers are currently telling us how this complexity and change can bring about a shock or sickness in the future. The "problem of the city," increasing bureaucracy and institutional complexity, social disorder and alienation, rising crime rates, and

[1]Roland L. Warren, *The Community in America* (Chicago: Rand McNally and Company, 1963), p. 9.

various other frustrations are evidence that social change is even now affecting all phases of life.

Two major changes that affect all communities and cause fragile and impersonal human ties are population growth and urbanization. Most population estimates indicate that in two decades, three at the most, another 100 million people will be residing in the United States. This will represent approximately a 50 percent increase in our present population.

This population is very mobile — most people moving to and between the larger cities. Nearly 70 percent of the American people live on about 1 percent of the land. Urbanization has taken place primarily in the past three decades. Consequently, all communities, cities, and states are experiencing a nightmarish task in finding resources, providing services, and managing resultant complex human relationships.

Another phenomenon related to population change and urbanization, and in many cases caused by these factors, is the technological revolution. All phases of society have been affected by the resulting changes. For example, it has increased specialization which has led to more and larger organizations, greater bureaucracy, and growing impersonalness between workers. Consequently, ties to a community for whatever reason are becoming slight or often only temporary and transitory.

A final complexity to be mentioned in relation to the changing community is the tremendous and rapid increase in organizations and groups. Today a person can belong to a number of local groups (the horizontal dimension). In addition, membership in state and national organizations is also quite common (the vertical dimension). The consolidated power of large organizations or groups is often central to getting things done. However, this situation often tends to weaken individual ties to a locality and makes understanding the nature of community more difficult.

What might the nature of the changing community become in the next several years? There is mounting evidence that communities will continue to change for some time. Some people suggest that we should build new communities in remote areas to accommodate the growing population. A recent government research project was launched for the planning of an experimental community to be possibly located in the Great Plains area. One quarter of a million people might live in such a technologically perfect setting, which would include a transparent dome two miles in diameter. A major problem is determining how to provide employment for this population.

Other "experts" have been advocating and building special satellite communities or suburbs surrounding large cities but connected to them by rapid transit systems and super expressways. Three of the more famous communities of this nature now in existence are the following: Reston, Virginia; Columbia, Maryland; and Litchfield Park, Arizona. Their unique features include special street plans that limit the need for automobiles, neighborhood or village centers within easy walking distance, and housing clustered around recreational centers. Some employment opportunities are provided within these satellite communities, but most residents who earn regular salaries must commute to large cities for work.

Some people see systems of cities (each system called a megalopolis) becoming tied together in huge population masses over a wide range of land. It is as though each city is an organism that continues to grow until it links with another to become one. Projection scientists suggest that megalopolises will stretch from San Diego to San Francisco, from Chicago to Detroit, and from Washington, D.C., to New York City. Many other such systems could develop in the next two or three decades.

Finally, there are those who suggest that the future of America lies only in the large cities. The small community is thought doomed because of diminishing employment opportunities. New York City's Mayor John Lindsay even advocated that the largest cities should become national cities or states in their own right. Whether this movement will take place for some time or ever is only a point of current discussion. However, continuing evidence can be found that cities receive a steady stream of people each year in addition to their internal population growth.

If cities do continue to grow, and it is suggested that they will, what can be done to make them better places in which to live? The present population densities of portions of the cities are not really very high. To be sure, there is overcrowding in the slum sections of cities, but this can be corrected. Wasted land can be found in all cities in the form of huge parking lots, public utility right of ways, and vacant eyesores. This land can be utilized in several ways. As a matter of fact, most authorities indicate that cities will find it much less expensive to expand inward rather than outward. Existing water, sewer, and electricity lines can be utilized and long-distance transportation schemes will not be so critically needed.

That is not to say that problems won't accompany the continual population growth of cities. Certainly these problems must be solved, but it is not our purpose here to discuss proposed solutions. However, what is to prevent, for example, schools from being built over parks, 30-story apartment complexes from being constructed that are self-contained (including educational and employment opportunities), and shopping centers from being constructed over city reservoirs. These things can and will happen, but they require careful and coordinated planning.

The person living in a rural or sparsely populated area might think that the foregoing discussion does not relate to his particular situation. However, the economy of the United States is tied closely to where-ever the country's population is concentrated. So we must be concerned with all types of locality bases and in learning how to solve the problems within each. Further, the discussion in the few preceding paragraphs was intended to illustrate that the modern community is a changing one. To understand how to live successfully with this change we must be aware of all possible developments.

WHY SHOULD YOU KNOW YOUR COMMUNITY

Knowing your community, the different ways in which people might think about what you call community, and how it is changing are important aspects of effective living. Whether you are a teacher, a student, or a lifetime resident of some community you are probably interested in a better life for yourself and others. Consequently, the remaining chapters will present and develop some concepts related to understanding how educational systems and communities fit together and how individuals and families can have a more effective role in this interdependent relationship.

There are many examples of people trying to have a role in local decision-making. The burning of school buses in Pontiac, Michigan, to prevent the cross-town busing of children is one rather violent example. San Francisco's Chinatown residents elected to keep their school-age children at home for several weeks as a protest over the same issue. They claimed that busing destroyed the rights of their children to an education which would include a local racial emphasis. Amish parents are still trying to win the permanent right for a religious emphasis to the education that their children receive. A better knowledge of how to work more effectively in the community might have prevented some of the sorrow and hard feelings that accompanied or will accompany these examples.

Certain public school problems will be common to or affect almost every community. Yet, although communities share many similarities, communities also share many dissimilarities. Thus, it becomes important to understand how to work and live effectively within any type of a community setting, especially in this mobile society where people frequently move from one area to another.

Factors such as mobility and rapid change mean that we can no longer treat each community as though it were not associated with the rest of society. We need to capitalize on any similarities and learn how to deal with dissimilarities. We need some modern theory for studying our changing community. The definition offered earlier and information in future chapters should provide some of the basics for this theory, especially as you develop an understanding of the sense of community and apply the information to your own situation.

A sense of community, whether it be horizontal, vertical, or both, is needed before the most effective educational program can be implemented. As a matter of fact, a disorganized community is often open to problems or exploitation by various forces. An illustration is the community that recently found itself paying triple the original estimate on the construction of a new high school because of strikes, materials delay, abnormally low bids, and contract irregularities. Perhaps an organized community effort could have forced some type of settlement and salvaged some scarce dollars for more pressing needs.

Each individual is the product of his community. His or her channels of communication are through the community setting. Whatever the aim of any program, access to each individual is through the community. This does not mean that the manipulation of man is included in this access route. Each community citizen must be respected as a person. It is hoped that any community effort will involve persons relating to each other in a broad and deeply human way.

Thus, as community leaders plan any programs of change, they need to decide whether the change will be through self-determination or whether it will be imposed. This is a basic philosophical question difficult to answer but one that must be faced. Knowing your community, its strengths and weaknesses, and your fellow resident should help you to determine your role in any community program.

Every community has some type of locality base, for there cannot be common living without some pattern of association that is horizontal in nature. In addition, there is also association that is vertical in nature or outward reaching beyond the local setting. These patterns of association are further complicated because the community in America is changing constantly. Consequently, a person must learn how to live and work effectively in his or her community setting. The remaining chapters will be devoted to developing some concepts and ideas essential to this learning endeavor.

SOME DEFINITIONS

Community—The organization of various social activities and units in such a manner that the daily living of a certain set of people is facilitated.

Gemeinschaft—Shared, intimate, and personal relationships built around the interdependence of primary social groups in a locality setting.

Gesellschaft—Impersonal, logical, and formally contracted associations between people who are independent from each other. Bureaucracy is a product of gesellschaft.

Horizontal Relationships—The association of one individual to another individual within the same locality such as a neighborhood or a city.

Locality Setting—A specific or recognizable geographic setting in which a group of people reside.

Vertical Relationships—The association of an individual to another individual or to a group based primarily on group membership affiliation. The affiliation might include membership outside of the locality setting.

SELECTED BIBLIOGRAPHY

ABRAHMSON, JULIA. *A Neighborhood Finds Itself.* New York: Harper & Bros., 1959. 334 pages. Appendixes. Bibliography. Index. The author, an employee of the community agency involved, describes the story of an innovative effort in a declining Chicago area to "fuse the challenges of Negro in-migration and conservation into the excitement faced with similar problems." Especially valuable is her very frank review of the various mistakes made by the quite successful Hyde Park-Kenwood community endeavor.

BIDDLE, WILLIAM W., and BIDDLE, LOUREIDE J. *The Community Development Process: The Rediscovery of Local Initiative.* New York: Holt, Rinehart, and Winston, Inc., 1965. 334 pages. Appendixes. Bibliography. Index. The authors are guided by the philosophy that community development is essentially human development. They identify the means by which citizens in the small towns and urban neighborhoods of America can be encouraged to take action in an attempt to improve their local situation and to create or reaffirm a sense of community.

SANDERS, IRWIN T. *Making Good Communities Better.* Lexington, Kentucky: University of Kentucky Press, 1953. 199 pages. Topical index. This book can be treated as a sort of handbook on the community with a series of short articles telling readers what they can do to improve their communities. Some sections covered include "What Makes a Good Community," "How Communities Show Differences," and "Procedures for Civic Leaders."

TOFFLER, ALVIN. *Future Shock.* New York: Random House, 1970. 505 pages. Bibliography. Index. This book is about today. It is about what is presently happening to people who are overwhelmed by change. The author explores how this change affects the communities in which we live, the organizations to which we belong, and our associations with one another. Some suggestions for coping with the rapidity of change are offered.

WARREN, ROLAND L. *The Community in America.* Chicago: Rand McNally & Company, 1963. 306 pages. Author index. Subject index. It is the thesis of the book that changes in community living include an increasing orientation of local organizations and individuals toward extra-community systems. The phenomenon has resulted in a corresponding decline in community cohesion and autonomy. Suggested are some community action models for dealing with the changes.

CHAPTER 2

The Activation of the Educative Community

CHANGES REQUIRED IN THE EDUCATIONAL SYSTEM

Man very early realized that education was important. Educating the young for survival and independence was carried out first in the home, then in the tribal or community setting, and then through the church. However, somewhere along this path of change, it was decided that learning had become too complicated for the family or the community to manage alone and education as a specialized community service was created.

That we now live in an age of rapid change has been said in many ways by many people. Change has become the only inevitability in history; therefore, we must learn to educate for change. However, the more it is assumed that continual education is essential to be able to cope with change, the more will be the requirement for specialized knowledge. This, too, has led to a tendency for the educational system to become highly specialized.

The transition of the school to a specialized, systematized institution has advantages, such as the development of a corps of highly trained professionals. Most schools have teachers, counselors, vocational experts, and curriculum specialists all working together to provide an extensive program of education, from kindergarten through high school (K-12). In addition, many schools employ specialists to work in such areas as special education, career education, early childhood education, and family living education.

Another advantage has been in gained knowledge about the educational process. For example, some teachers use individualized curricula and methods in an attempt to help children achieve to the limits of their potential. Furthermore, audio-visual equipment, flexible scheduling, and work-study programs have been employed increasingly by various schools to supplement the learning process.

Despite the above and other advantages, however, education still requires some changes if the needs of all people are to be met. The school must be a place where young people are prepared for life roles, not a place isolated from the main current of life where students spend several years concentrating primarily on subject content. Thus, education should be person-centered, problem-oriented, and community-centered. However, changes in the school as we now know it will be successful only to the point that members of the supportive community share in attempts to redefine the tasks. In addition current constraints, such as limited finances and large classes, will need to be dealt with.

The teacher, too, needs to support any changes in the educational system, and, perhaps, be changed with it. Some critics accuse teachers of being subject-oriented rather than people-oriented or community-oriented. Other critics suggest that teachers' interests are directed only upward within the bureaucracy of the school system itself. The point is that the educational system will require financial support adequate enough to attract and hold the best possible teachers and administrators. Without continued professional excellence and educators committed to making the school an integral part of the community, attempts to increase the school's community commitment will be futile. (Chapter 8 will delve into the teacher-training situation as it relates to preparing educators for commitment to community education.)

How are the schools doing today in their attempts to promote social change or in their attempts to develop citizens capable of survival in rapid change, especially in large cities? Some people suggest that the schools have not succeeded as well as they could. Innovations such as programmed instruction, new scheduling techniques, and non-graded classes are felt to be mere window dressings of a system that is out of date.

There is growing evidence that the schools have not had major success in equipping the disadvantaged members of society with the skills and knowledge needed for effective living. It is not our purpose to discuss various reasons for this lack of success. Rather, we are suggesting that because every person normally spends a great deal of his or her early life in school, the education received should be adequate enough to provide for most normal needs.

The fault for most present school limitations centers not only on the educational system and its staff. Many forces have emerged that make the educational task a difficult one. Such factors as drug problems, youth's changing attitudes, and society's changing values have all contributed to the complexity of providing an education that is useful and relevant. Furthermore, the rapidity of technological advance has created what some scholars refer to as a wide cultural lag. The inability to fill this gap through training or education has contributed to a situation where community needs and educational goals are often out of harmony.

Our definition of community noted that those social units performing societal functions must be combined to serve the needs of a given public. The school is one of these major units. Unfortunately, too often the school has become separated from other community institutions, many of which also have educational functions. The school can no longer afford to remain autonomous or separate from the community, its citizens, and its various institutions. The school and the community must learn to reinforce each other in teaching about life and about living with social change.

The local public normally has very few avenues for its voice to be heard in relation to education. The feeling that others are constantly making decisions for or about him is prevalent among many citizens. Thus, there needs to be developed a mechanism whereby the school and the citizen can work together for the mutual betterment of the community.

A CASE FOR DECENTRALIZATION OF EDUCATIONAL DECISION-MAKING

One frequently mentioned precondition for greater community and citizen participation in the educational process is decentralization of the public schools. Particularly in the large cities, this is often seen as a vital need. In Detroit, Michigan, for example, decentralization was accomplished by a state legislative act. The purpose of the plan was to spread the decision-making base from 5 persons to 45 persons, 40 of whom represent eight different regions of the larger city.

Decentralization often is thought to include only some legal or highly formalized arrangement for involving the local citizen in educational decision-making. However, decentralization can be a matter of mind in addition to, or in lieu of, being a matter of fact. If a person believes that the local school is serving his needs or that the average citizen can have a part in the determination of policy, then decentralization has been accomplished. Thus, decentralization can take place in small or large communities, and it can be made formal or can happen informally.

If we assume that the decentralization movement will help both large and small cities to bring resources to bear on educational needs, the following could be products:

1. The provision of a vehicle by which the total community engages in democratic decision-making.
2. The development of better relationships between the school system and the community.
3. The implementation of a continuous evaluation of need to provide feedback information for educational planning.
4. The evolvement of the school as a vital part, but only one part, of a whole community process of education.

The greater involvement of the community in education, and, indeed, the success of decentralization attempts, rests on the premise that the school will serve the particular needs of the clientele it serves rather than some general set of requirements established at a centralized level. Many experts suggest that decentralization of schools will begin to meet these particular needs. For example, a large city such as Los Angeles might implement alternative school programs for its various ethnic or racial areas if the concept of involving local residents in local decision-making was followed.

Perhaps the most widely known and discussed plan for the decentralization of educational decision-making was proposed for New York City. The Bundy Report—as the New York study is commonly called—proposed that 60 or more autonomous school districts be set up in the city, each representing a distinct community or locality. Each school district would be controlled by parent-dominated school boards. Thus, the goal is that each local community will be large enough to effectively carry out the necessary educational functions and services, yet small enough to be sensitive to the unique needs of the local clientele.

Supreme Court rulings have added a complexity to helping local community residents feel that education is meeting their needs. However, it is suggested that even the busing of children to schools away from the local community, one of the issues brought about by a court ruling, does not prohibit two communities from working together on a coordinated school plan. Furthermore, the fact remains that the local school building is still part of the local community and can serve many useful functions.

Federal legislation is even being proposed that would give national recognition to the idea of community education and the local school as a center for various community activities. Consequently, it is suggested that all means to involve local residents with the schools will be useful in promoting a sense of community between educator and citizen.

Is there reason to believe that greater community involvement in the public schools will improve the educational system? The findings of the much-discussed Coleman Report of the 1960s suggest that the answer is yes. In this report, which examined the equality of educational opportunity, it was found that the most important need in an educational system was to promote a strong sense of worth among the students. What better way of starting this than with parents and students having some self-determination of their own destinies through helping to make local educational decisions.

There will be problems in implementing a greater decentralization of the public schools. In addition, when something new or different leads to educational changes, there is no guarantee of improvements in the educational system. To obtain some understanding of all the problems and potential changes, the reader is urged to explore various current issues of the periodicals listed at the conclusion of this chapter.

One basic problem might well be a hesitation on the part of professional educators to give up their relatively autonomous decision-making roles. Administrators and board members might question the ability of the community citizen to understand fully various educational needs and problems. Community leaders and other citizens, in turn, will be unsure of how they can work with educators. However, it is anticipated that once the community member and educator begin to work more closely with each other, the educational system and its participants will reap increased benefits.

Furthermore, the decentralization issue and the greater involvement of local residents in education must be examined in light of several factors in the United States. There is still a widening economic gap between the rich and the poor; evidence is available that the polarization between black and white continues to increase; the desegregation of public schools is still incomplete; and the increased intolerance and lack of cooperation among many groups of people have created new community tensions.

To successfully educate all people we must remove from our society those conditions that prevent adequate learning, such as ghettos, segregation, unemployment, and inadequate income. We can't afford to use community involvement as an issue by which the various educational and social problems are dumped off for solution by local leadership. The need is to educate all people for social action.

The educational professional, the community citizen, and the public policy-maker must all work together to help the school become a better institution.

The school is one facility that exists in almost all communities. It is also the only public agency that exists in neighborhoods or locality bases throughout the United States. Furthermore, the educational system is the one remaining public unit that is common to all groups in our society. We need to capitalize on this similarity between communities.

The school can help in different ways in different communities; but that is a potential strength and at the center of a greater utilization of the educational system. Learning how to involve local citizens in educational decision-making, developing new roles for the educational system, and discovering how to activate the entire community in problem-solving are skills educators must obtain. A greater utilization of the community and its people may be our best chance to solve the many problems facing current society.

DEVELOPING A SENSE OF COMMUNITY

We have discussed some of the changes required for the educational system in America. We have also discussed the need for community participation in decision-making if a greater utilization of education to solve local problems is to be realized. Now let us examine how a greater sense of community can be developed in people as a prerequisite to creating an educative community.

A person is a product of his community. Learning to live and work effectively in a community setting is especially important in view of the rapidity of social change. The first chapter described how social change is a force contributing to people forming more and more vertical associations, a situation tending to weaken ties to a locality setting. Consequently, developing a greater sense of community requires that horizontal relationships be strengthened wherever possible.

We have suggested that joint planning between community citizens and school officials will facilitate attempts to activate the entire community in an educational sense. It is also suggested that community involvement in educational decision-making—through decentralized local involvement and/or some other means—will contribute to the strengthening of horizontal ties and to developing a greater sense and understanding of community.

Various means of involving parents and citizens in community and educational programs are being tried in several American communities. Block clubs, community councils, advisory boards, and ad hoc problem-solving committees are typical of these means. Consultation and appraisal of school programs, often in concert with school officials or educational specialists, can do much to facilitate an understanding of educational needs and problems. Perhaps personnel in the educational system will need to provide leadership training to in turn receive assistance in problem-solving from the community. It is expected that a person's sense of community will be heightened as he becomes more able to assist with various community problems.

The educational system in a community must give people opportunities to become more active citizens. There are many ways a school can enlist the support and cooperation of parents and other citizens of the community. Regularly scheduled parent-teacher conferences are a beginning step. Parents and other interested citizens may also serve in many volunteer roles, from being a band booster to being a class sponsor. Many schools are also finding roles for the paid aide or paraprofessional. All of these possibilities may initially present problems in role conflict or expectations, but they do provide opportunities for people normally outside the school system to feel a part of an important aspect of their community life.

Students, too, can be given opportunities to practice their community citizenship, for example, a year of service for high school students, with credit, for working on various community needs such as community action programs or volunteer work. Students could also act as tutors for younger, educationally disadvantaged students. A school might offer physical education credit to high school students who would spend a few hours each week leading recreational activities for senior citizens. Elementary and junior high school students could also contribute to the community by becoming involved with community ecology projects.

Teachers should also be encouraged and given time to participate in community activities. Home visits to various kinds of family environments could provide a better understanding of certain community and student needs. Teachers might also provide leadership skills on various community improvement projects. Helping people learn to solve problems can take place anywhere in a community setting.

The school and its personnel can be the central forces in helping people to develop a sense of community and a sense of their own potential to solve problems. Chapter 3 describes in greater detail the use of the school as a community school and the various roles the school can play in a community. Through a community education approach, all resources in a community are potential learning forces and factors. Activating these resources seems imperative if the needs of societies and communities are to be met.

ACTIVATING THE ENTIRE COMMUNITY

The concept of activating the educative community, as the title of this chapter suggests, assumes that most persons and agencies in a community have a potential if not actual capacity for being involved in the educational process. More importantly, it is suggested that these persons and agencies should assume some responsibility for the educational function. This will necessitate some changes in the educational system. Schools, however, will still have a responsibility to the total community, regardless of whether the decisions affecting them come from a centralized source or from some scheme involving local citizen participation.

It is the thesis of this chapter, and of the whole book for that matter, that the community is a teacher of all the people who live there. The community is a teacher or a school in the sense that it is the setting in which people's attitudes, talents, and behaviors are influenced. It should be the obligation of the educational system, and primarily the school, to help the community become a better teacher. The community, the people, and the schools will need to interact for the betterment of all.

In the truly educative community, all individuals will accept that the education of the young is a task requiring time and energy on the part of each member of the community. Education then becomes distinguishable and different from schooling. The schools do not become irrelevant under this premise; they actually must play vital roles in coordinating all educative activities and might even assume new roles. Furthermore, the humanistic intents of educational professionals can begin to be separated from the rules and traditions of the confined school building.

Through this approach to education and learning—what we referred to in the previous section as the community education approach—all resources in the community are viewed as potential learning forces and factors. This also may be viewed as attempts to strengthen the horizontal relationships of citizens to their communities. The people and facilities of the community's schools join together with the resources and talents of the community and its residents. This way a school can operate effectively with local control and each school's educational program can reflect the community in which it exists.

Education is the sum of many parts, including not only what is available through the school program, but also through the home, the church, the peer group, and the community. Each person is reached through some aspect of the community in which he resides. Thus, once this is realized, it becomes important for each educator to obtain and analyze various kinds of community information. Understanding the child to be educated, including his family background, and the needs of the community is only a partial suggestion of the necessary information. Various sources at the conclusion of this chapter will give additional insights on the subject.

The discussion thus far has perhaps seemed somewhat idealistic. However, if all the people in the United States are going to be served and be given an equal opportunity for an adequate preparation for life, the educational system will need to change to meet the challenge.

Becoming a part of a larger educative community will mean some new and even expanded roles for the school. The basic purpose of the school will still be the improvement of the society, the community, and the individual. However, this might mean that in addition to classroom instruction, some teachers will become change agents, some will become ombudsmen (see definition, end of chapter), some will work to improve school and community relations, and others will work at developing community leadership.

The school will not forsake learning as an objective, as a community's development is in a large part dependent on education. But, it is suggested that we need to help our youth learn more *from* the world than just always *about* it. Furthermore, the educational system could use its knowledge base and professionals' skills on various community improvement tasks involving the schools, the teachers, the students, and the community residents. The schools would play an important role by helping community residents recognize and carry out various responsibilities. The school, then, would reach into every corner of its community, touch every citizen, rejuvenate community pride, and serve as a facilitating agent in helping people to help themselves.

Education is important and vital from the cradle to the grave; it is never too late to learn more about helping yourself. Thus, schools can play a crucial community role by offering adult education activities designed to help residents meet some of their needs. Chapter 7 discusses more thoroughly why communities need adult and continuing education activities.

The school also can play an important role as a center for neighborhood and community life. The community center idea utilizes existing educational facilities to meet the needs of all ages and groups in the local area. Chapter 3 discusses the community center concept as one important aspect of the community school.

What, then, is needed as schools, teachers, and parents strive to use more fully the entire community? A crucial need is learning how to communicate with all elements of the community. This means school personnel should know how to communicate with students, parents, and other community residents from a variety of socioeconomic backgrounds. It also means that community residents are encouraged to communicate their problems and needs to educators. Chapter 5 discusses communication needs in greater detail.

Another need is to bring together all the learning forces and factors available for purposes of teaching, learning, and problem-solving. An important aspect of this need is to learn how to use all the talents and skills of the teachers in a community, rather than assign them only to classroom teaching. Teachers may need to be trained to be more aware of the community, to be able to survey community needs, and to know better how to deal with community and societal change. (Chapter 8 examines some of the teacher-training needs associated with the educative community concept.) Why shouldn't an English teacher, for example, become involved with the development of reading programs for senior citizens?

Release time from classroom instruction and some increased financial support will be required for the teacher to play three important roles in the educative community: instructor, curriculum developer (using some of the resources of the community), and liaison with the community. However, by getting out into the community as a liaison or to develop educational curricula, the teacher will learn more about the community and, thereby, should be able to improve his or her instructional endeavors.

Parents, too, will need to play an important part in activating the educative community. Parents who are not involved, who do not know what is taking place in the school, can certainly not reinforce what the school is doing with their children. Parents and other citizens can help plan educational curricula. Parents can be taught how to use the community and its services for supplementing their children's education. A greater involvement of parents in the educational process through existing or new organizations will hopefully raise their aspirations and leadership skills, and, in turn, positively affect their children.

Other recognized educational agencies should be encouraged to play a larger role in the educative community. Private schools, libraries, museums, and such media as newspapers, radio, and television are those common to most communities. Their contributions could become more explicit, systematic, and extensive.

The community college is yet another educational institution that should be mentioned. More and more communities in America are building community colleges. Their function potentially can go far beyond the central campus. In addition to the facilities and staff available to the local community, most community colleges are making an increased effort to provide various services to the community. Those communities possessing such a facility must work to make it an important part of the total educational process.

Churches, too, can play an important educational role. For example, churches might provide weekend retreats for engaged or married couples where an exploration of family life relationships could take place. Churches could also serve as sites for, and provide the leadership for, discussions by teenagers on drug problems, sexuality, and inter-family relationships.

We have attempted to build the case that the entire community is potentially a living learning laboratory. The community provides every variety of human function, every example of human association, every technological process, and every type of building or facility. Consequently, schools should draw upon the community for a large measure of their curricula.

Learners could go out to all parts of the community, where various facilities can be shared, resource persons can be utilized, and most importantly, scarce financial support for education can be used as efficiently as possible. In this situation YMCA and YWCA sites are used for physical education classes; the public library becomes a media and book center; the parks are recreation centers; zoos, museums, and art galleries become actual examples for various subject areas, and business and industry settings become the bases for career education. Appendix A gives various examples of supplemental experiences for different curricular areas.

Extending the school to the whole community can affect the entire family. Parents should be encouraged to take educational tours and trips with their children as a way of reinforcing the learning. Community service projects around local community problems can involve both parent and child. School leaders could even develop parent guide material that would describe potential educational opportunities and how to help children utilize them.

Utilizing the community as a learning laboratory will take careful planning and coordination. The various community activities and examples suggested above will not be very effective in promoting learning if they are not integrated with school activities. This reinforces an earlier suggestion that educator and parent must plan the educational program together. The community belongs to all its residents; activating the education will take careful planning and dedication.

We have not discussed how activating the educative community can be financed. Future study and experience should begin to reveal what changes, personnel, and costs will be required. Hopefully, the various requirements will not be extensive and community residents will feel that a greater community participation in education is worth supporting. The following chapter describes the community school, a vehicle used by some communities to activate the educative community and to facilitate the finding of resources necessary for this activation.

APPENDIX A*

Supplemental Community Experience for Various Curricular Areas

Language Arts

1. A community-wide book fair to encourage reading and the use of books.
2. Students meeting periodically in the home of a Spanish-speaking family for purposes of conversational Spanish and examining another culture.
3. The public library promotes a greater use of its books and media to encourage and establish habits toward a continuing practice of self-inquiry.

Science

1. Parents and students develop a basement laboratory to supplement and encourage learning about the sciences.
2. Students and teachers regularly visit local chemical, electrical, and other science-related industries to examine the application of science principles and techniques.
3. Scientists, engineers, and medical professionals visit the classrooms to describe their professions and to teach certain parts of the science subjects.

*Ideas for this section came from the first in a series of booklets being prepared on community education. See W. Fred Totten and Frank J. Manley, *The Community Education Concept and Nature and Function of the Community School.* Unit 101 (Flint, Michigan: W. Fred Totten, 1810 Ramsay Boulevard, 1970).

4. Parents and students plan and carry out some local ecology project. The students receive school credit and/or time off to complete the projects.

Music and Art

1. Parents and students are encouraged to participate together in community bands, choirs, or art classes to create a greater interest in, and appreciation for, music or art.
2. Students, parents, and teachers attend community concerts or art shows together to enhance an interest in music or art.

Health and Safety

1. Family life-study courses are developed for parents to help them better understand how to reinforce education and learning in the home.
2. A community campaign on safe driving is organized jointly by parents and students.
3. Parents assist with sight and hearing examinations of students to better understand various student health needs.

Social Studies

1. A course centered on "Understand Our Community" is developed for joint participation by parents and students to help them learn how the community and schools both educate people.
2. A teen traffic court is established to give students some practical knowledge and experience with court procedures.

Homemaking

1. A program on family life and human relationship is sponsored by the community council of churches. The program participants are engaged or young married couples and the resource personnel are various church and school professionals.
2. A breakfast program for low-income students is implemented by homemaking students and parents.
3. Clothing selection and construction and/or food and nutrition projects for both daughter and mother are organized and administered by the homemaking instructors.

SOME DEFINITIONS

Community Education — This can be thought of as a way of viewing education in the locality setting, a means by which people, their problems, and community resources are central to designing an educational program. The traditional role of the school is expanded to one of identifying needs, problems, and concerns of the community and then assisting in the development and utilization of programs toward improving the entire community.

Community School—A site serving as a center for community education. Sometimes referred to as the "lighted school house," the community school attempts to facilitate education to all groups of people at all times of the day and year.

Educative Community—That community which is a learning laboratory in its totality.

Ombudsman—An individual appointed or elected to handle grievances against local governmental officials. This person will investigate complaints, intervene on behalf of citizens, and mediate local disputes but remains independent of both citizen and government.

SELECTED BIBLIOGRAPHY

Books

HICKEY, HOWARD W.; VAN VOORHEES, CURTIS; and ASSOCIATES. *The Role of the School in Community Education.* Midland, Michigan: Pendell Publishing Company, 1969. 133 pages. Selected bibliography. The book discusses the organization, staffing, program planning, financing, facilities, and evaluation required for a community education program centered on the community school. It is written for teachers, students in community education, school officials, and parents.

IRWIN, MARTHA, and RUSSELL, WILMA. *The Community Is the Classroom.* Midland, Michigan: Pendell Publishing Company, 1971. 131 pages. Bibliography. The authors have documented examples and experiences that show the possibilities of utilizing the community as an open classroom. Chapters center on developing community-centered curriculum. Teachers, administrators, and concerned parents are the proposed audience for the book.

KERENSKY, VASIL M., and MELBY, ERNEST O. *Education II—The Social Imperative.* Midland, Michigan: Pendell Publishing Company, 1971. 192 pages. Bibliography. Centering on the challenges of education in the urban community and with the disadvantaged, the authors propose that education for all people is feasible and possible, provided we better utilize the resources and knowledge already available. The authors also examine the utilization of various community resources.

OLSEN, EDWARD G. *The School and Community Reader: Education in Perspective.* New York: The Macmillan Company, 1963. 523 pages. Index. Sources. A collection of readings on the practice, methods, and theory dealing with the school and the community. This book covers topics dealing with the use of community resources, meeting the community's needs, working with community leaders, and developing the education-centered community.

SUMPTION, MERLE R., and ENGSTROM, YVONNE. *School-Community Relations: A New Approach.* New York: McGraw-Hill Book Company, 1966. 238 pages. Index. Appendix. This book attempts to treat the community as an active participant with the school in education. The role of the community in educational endeavors, how the school and community work together, and the school in the power structure are some of the topics covered.

TOTTEN, W. FRED. *The Power of Community Education.* Midland, Michigan: Pendell Publishing Company, 1970. 168 pages. Index. Bibliography. This book is designed primarily for teachers and administrators wishing for a broad overview of the community education theory and how it can be used to solve various community problems. Included are case examples to illustrate the various topics.

Periodicals

The Bulletin of the National Association of Secondary School Principals. Published nine times each year by the National Association of Secondary School Principals, Washington, D.C. Contains articles related to community education and other educational issues.

Community Education Journal. Published quarterly by the Pendell Company, Midland, Michigan. The journal centers on community education and the community schools, but also includes various articles on educational issues.

The Community School and Its Administration. Published monthly by the Inter-Institutional Workshop in cooperation with the Flint Board of Education and the Mott Foundation of Flint, Michigan. Articles center on community education, the community schools, and current educational issues.

Current. Published monthly by Goddard Publications, Inc., Plainfield, Vermont. The periodical often contains current articles related to the urban community or school.

Harvard Educational Review. Published quarterly by an Editorial Board of Graduate Students in Harvard University, Cambridge, Massachusetts. The journal often contains articles related to community education.

Phi Delta Kappan. Published monthly by Phi Delta Kappa, Inc., Bloomington, Indiana. The periodical contains articles related to current issues in education.

Teachers College Record. Published quarterly by the Teachers College, Columbia University, New York. The journal contains current articles on various educational topics.

CHAPTER 3

The Community School

THE COMMUNITY SCHOOL – CENTER OF COMMUNITY EDUCATION

Developing a sense of community and activating the educative community are important preludes to the community education process. In this process we think of the community as belonging to all the people who reside there. The people, their problems, and the total community resources become central to all educational programs. The community's schools serve as centers for education; their programs are directed toward improving the entire community.

Community education is basically a concept. This concept involves all the people of a locality and assumes that the whole society is or can be engaged in the process of education. Thus, if we accept that the school does belong to all the people, we must take a wider view that schools can effectively serve people in more ways than just K-12 schooling. This means better utilization of the untapped skills and resources in the community and making better use of unused and available school space and equipment.

The community education concept also implies that education will have an impact upon the locality it serves. The successful community education program will reflect the unique nature of the community it serves and will meet the needs of all residents. This means, as we noted in the preceding chapter, that citizens need to become involved in the decisions affecting the school and its programs.

A philosophy that accompanies the community education process is that learning is a continuous, lifelong experience and need. This implies a process that begins in the home at birth, is continued in the community school, and is perpetuated in the educative community throughout one's life. Later chapters build on this philosophy.

The development of continuous learning efforts is based on utilizing the total community as a teacher. Because the neighborhood

33

school is a common denominator of community life for most people, it can be utilized as a vehicle for the planning, organization, and implementation of educational programs relevant to the entire community.

The public schools have a capacity for greater leadership and utilization than most are now experiencing. For example, schools could take the lead in building community solidarity. The school also could become the center of educational service for people of all ages. In its ultimate goal, the school seeks to influence the community toward constructive change by assisting community residents to solve various problems basic to community living.

In a traditional view, the school is limited primarily to the facilitation of academic learning through day programs for children and youth. The broader view of school being promoted in this chapter —the community school— suggests quite a different approach to education. The community school is usually open many hours each day and school personnel work to help both youth and adults in solving various community and social problems.

It will be the purpose of this chapter to present the community school as an important part of the community education process. The community school concept has evolved from utilizing the school as a center for recreation to the school as a center of community development and change. The community and its schools must become interdependent if education is to help meet the many needs of a modern, changing society.

THE COMMUNITY SCHOOL—PAST AND PRESENT

The community school movement had its beginning in Flint, Michigan. Between 1932 and 1935, Flint was experiencing several kinds of problems. The community depended a great deal on the auto industry and economic hard times were affecting many residents. Some left the community in search of work and others moved in hoping to find jobs. This instability of population made it difficult to obtain a stabilized educational program.

An unstable educational system meant little financial support for the schools. A minimal service was provided students; obtaining money for new facilities was virtually impossible. Teacher salaries were also low, resulting in many fine teachers leaving the community.

Related to the educational situation was the beginning of several community problems. The incidence of juvenile delinquency was rising, often resulting in property damage to school and other community buildings. In addition, minority and poor people were often out of work or employed only part of the time, leading to community tensions and uneasiness.

Mr. Charles Stewart Mott, who had been mayor of Flint and long active in various community affairs, was troubled by the problems in his adopted home. Mr. Mott had moved to Flint in 1907 to establish a supportive industry for auto manufacturers. He later owned many shares in a leading auto company and established a philanthropic foundation for purposes of helping American communities in their growth and development.

When Mr. Frank Manley, physical education and recreation supervisor in the Flint public schools, presented some ideas on how the school could begin to solve various community problems, Mr. Mott agreed to help. Thus, in 1935 the Mott Foundation contributed an initial $6,000 to the Flint Public Schools for purposes of a greater utilization of the school facilities and the community school concept was born.

The community school concept is often used synonymously with several terms: "the open-door policy," "the lighted school house," and "the neighborhood school." The neighborhood school or community school is simply a school within easy access of local residents; access meaning a close proximity to where people live, a school open most hours of the year, and educational programs designed for, and in cooperation with, the residents.

Figure 1 illustrates the community school concept and how local residents can have an impact on the educational services provided by schools. This illustration displays the community as a locality setting, with schools having a horizontal relationship to each other and to the citizens of the community.

Educational services and programs are developed according to need and interest. Assuming that the community school is serving as one center for various educational programs in a community and that local citizens have been utilized for purposes of planning programs, the illustration can explain how the programs are designed. For example, a local boy scout troup needs a site for their meetings and activities. A community elementary school—the figure shows one such school surrounded by bold-lined arrows—could serve as such a site. Any of the other community elementary schools might be used in a similar manner.

Another example in a truly educative community might be that several mothers and daughters are working together on a clothing buymanship project in the late afternoons. The illustration shows with

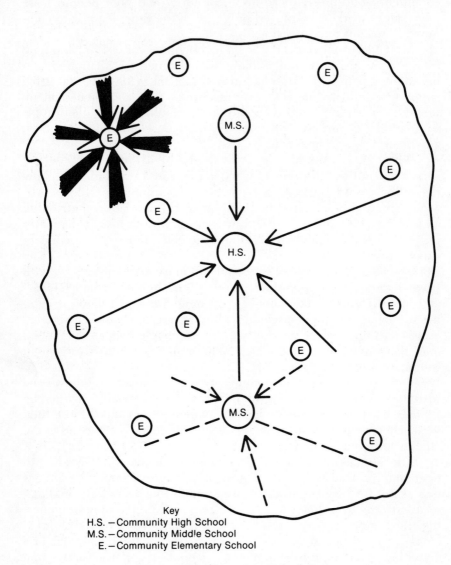

Key
H.S. — Community High School
M.S. — Community Middle School
 E. — Community Elementary School

Figure 1. The Community School Concept

dotted lined arrows several daughters and mothers coming to a community middle school for instruction by a teacher of home economics in the middle school. The participants and instructor might use the school facilities for most of the educational project but could also share transportation for supplemental field trips to stores in local suburbs or to the central city.

The interest in or need for the above project might not have been great enough to have such a project in one or more of the elementary schools, but the middle school serves as a central site for a larger area without participants having to commute all the way across a large community for the educational service. In our illustrated community, such a buymanship project could be held in both middle schools if the interest was great enough.

A final example from Figure 1 centers upon the use of the community high school. In our hypothetical community let's assume that various residents expressed a desire to hear and see some of the currently popular nonfiction authors. The community high school could serve as a central location for presentations by some authors invited to the city. In the figure this is illustrated by single-line arrows representing people coming to the high school from various parts of the community.

When the community school concept or philosophy is fully implemented, citizens contribute in many ways to the school programs and to the solving of various community problems. This participation involves four "ins":

IN — Get the people of the community into the schools, initially by means of educational opportunities based on their immediate needs.
INTERESTED — Get them interested in their own problems and the problems of the community.
INFORMED — Help people become informed on how problems can be solved and why the responsible citizen should be concerned with community improvement.
INVOLVED — Ask people to help and to assume leadership roles in various educational endeavors directed toward solving community problems.

In Flint, Michigan, citizen participation through the community schools has grown steadily since that initial $6,000 investment. Each year nearly 100,000 children and adults, out of a population of approximately 250,000, are involved in a variety of educational programs ranging from regular and experimental K-12 programs to adult education activities to community recreation programs.

The community school idea has grown far beyond the boundaries of Flint, Michigan. More than 300 communities in the United States and other countries have initiated community school programs in their own school systems. The Mott Foundation has also helped to establish several regional and university centers for community school development. These centers were provided to give assistance and direction in further developing community education and the community school concept around the country.

Perhaps the clearest indication of the continual expansion of the community school idea is the recent attention given to community education by state and federal legislation. Various currently funded acts — ranging from the Adult Education Act to the Model Cities Programs to the Vocational Education Act — can be utilized in many ways to benefit community school programs. In addition, Florida, for example, passed the Florida Community School Act in 1970. The purpose of the act is to provide state leadership and financial support in establishing community schools. Maryland, Michigan, Minnesota, Utah, and Washington also have recently adopted similar legislation. Other states are considering legislation to support community schools.

Most important, though, federal legislation strictly for community education has been introduced in both the House of Representatives and the Senate. For example, the Senate bill, called the "Community School Center Development Act," is designed to promote the development and expansion of community schools in all 50 states. This legislation, if funded, should provide support to initiate community school programs wherever they are needed.

THE ADMINISTRATION OF COMMUNITY SCHOOLS

Administering community schools is not the same as administering traditional schools. Many of the management principles are the same, but the community school administrator, director, or teacher must develop a sixth sense about the community in which the school exists. Involving students, parents, and other citizens in program-planning and implementation, offering the school as a center for various community activities, and diagnosing community needs all require an expanded approach to organizing and operating school programs.

Staffing Needs

The staff requirements for a community school program vary some, although not extensively, from those for a more traditional school. Often, when implementing the community school concept, the same staff members can be utilized; however, their training requirements and the responsibilities assumed can differ significantly.

The superintendent, for example, must be skilled at short- and long-range educational planning and evaluation that involves not only the K-12 programs but also the relationship of the school to the educational needs of the total community. He or she becomes the overall manager of the educative community. One current training mechanism for community school superintendents is the Mott Internship Program in Flint. Chapter 8 discusses more thoroughly the need for higher education to prepare administrators and teachers who can work effectively in community schools.

The building principal in a community school also performs a different role than in the traditional school. Perhaps as much as one-half of the community school principal's time is involved in establishing and administering educational programs related to the community. This could involve developing a coordinated effort between the school and various community agencies; it could involve home visitations with teachers and counselors to determine what is needed to help youngsters become better learners; and it could include the establishment of educational experiences and opportunities throughout the community for citizens to become involved in. The responsibility in the school building becomes one of coordinating and guiding in-class instruction, rather than just monitoring instruction and student progress.

The community school requires an administrative staff to handle various functions. Such tasks as in-service education for staff, record-keeping, report-writing, public relations, working with problem children, and routine administrative operations should be handled by specialists, consultants, and administrative assistants, so the superintendent and principal can have additional time to spend in the community. These staff members would report to the superintendent or to building principals.

The community school teacher will also perform somewhat different roles. He or she will relate much more closely what happens in the classroom to the home and to the community. Some teachers will visit homes to better determine and understand educational needs. Other teachers will work with parents and students in supplemental educational activities in the home and in the community. Other teachers will have at least a partial assignment working with adult and community education activities. Finally, some teachers will assume leadership roles over groups of teachers, paraprofessionals, and volunteers, probably in a single curricular area, to bring direction to the total educational efforts. If teachers are not specifically trained by universities to perform in these roles, in-service training through the schools will probably be necessary.

Various paraprofessional and volunteer roles nicely supplement community school programs. For example, in Flint there is emerging a role for the paraprofessional school-community aide. After receiving the necessary training, these persons work primarily with lower socio-economic families on such topics as nutrition education and child care education. There are many other roles paraprofessionals can assume, ranging from assisting with Head Start programs to being teacher aides in the classroom. Direction and training will usually be provided by professional school personnel.

The counselor or counseling staff plays an important role in the implementation of community school programs. Not only do counselors need to be trained to diagnose, prescribe, and evaluate educational programs, but they also need to relate closely to the home and community environments. Home visitations, counseling with parents, and consultation with teachers should be a regular part of the counseling function. Counselors also should be equipped to help teachers and administrators learn how to deal with special problems of youth and parents. Finally, counselors should be able to develop career education programs to match both societal needs and student interests and abilities.

The reorganization of a traditional school system into a community school program will not require the instant employment of a large new staff. Often personnel already employed will simply be trained for and fulfill new roles. However, a community school system requires support by various auxiliary personnel. These personnel will come in part from similar positions or out-dated positions; others will need to be newly employed, especially if the program grows. In Flint, for example, supportive staff positions such as community school nurse, librarian, medical specialists, police-school liaison officer, and adult education specialists are in existence. Flint's large adult education and recreation programs alone employ a staff of several hundred administrators, workers, and teachers.

An important need in modern communities is adaptation to constant social change. The community schools could facilitate this adaptation by adding a person, or persons, specially trained to deal with change to the staff. Such experts, sometimes called change agents, could provide coordination for the various social action programs in a community. The change specialist could also work to build community understanding and support of education in the schools and in the total community. Perhaps such a person could work to involve the school in community development and improvement projects. In situations where community schools employed such personnel, roles would undoubtedly evolve differently for each community.

A final staffing need to be discussed here is that of the community school director. This is perhaps the most important position for the success of any community school program. The Mott Internship Program and the Flint Community Schools currently provide most of the training and preparation of community school directors through six-week workshops held throughout the year or through a year-long internship program.

The community school director is usually a qualified teacher whose day begins typically at noon. The director will usually teach some classes in the afternoon and/or direct some recreational activities. He or she also directs the after-school and evening activities. This means involvement in adult education, senior citizen activities, retraining programs, and service organizations for children and adults.

Community school directors need to be especially tuned to the educational needs and interests of the families living within the boundaries of the school to which they are assigned. The community school director will utilize various kinds of inputs to determine what educational programs and services will best fulfill local needs, and he must be skilled at evaluation, public relations, and communications.

Program Options

There is a variety of educational programs and activities that can be developed in the community schools. They can be designed as a supplement to the regular day program for children or as extracurricular activities outside the regular school hours. They can be developed for youth, parent, and other community residents. The programs and activities developed over many years in the Flint community schools will be used as examples in the following discussion.

Enriching the curriculum of the daytime program for youth can be accomplished in a variety of ways. Arts and crafts, breakfast and lunch programs, creative dramatics, health clinics, puppetry, and sunrise singing are some of the activities that could be included in the community school program with cooperation from the educative community. Flint has also developed and added such curriculum-related programs as special help for the inner city child, the personalized curriculum program for potential dropouts, the Mott farm program for visitation and study, and special programs for physically handicapped youngsters.

The community school concept also provides a unique opportunity for youth through late-afternoon or weekend activities. Recreational programs, supplemental instruction, cultural activities, and hobby classes can be made available after the regular school session. The Flint community schools cooperate with character-building activities such as 4-H, Big Brothers, Stepping Stone program (for girls), Scouts, Gra-Y, and the police-school cadet program for elementary and junior high boys.

Evening activities are another important part of the community school program. Adults and teens are the primary participants. Teen clubs, parent-child activities, recreational activities, and adult education classes can be organized. The Flint adult education program, for example, includes such courses or activities as Adult Basic Education, high school completion, typing, antique finishing, knitting, quality dressmaking, oil painting, expectant couples classes, lecture-discussion programs, and senior citizen programs. Some communities even offer adult education programs 24 hours a day for people who work early evening or night shifts.

Many communities currently have large adult education programs offering courses and activities similar to those described above. This will provide a good start if the community school concept is implemented. However, the Flint experiences have shown that evening activities must be based on the expressed or determined needs of community residents if successful participation is to be continually obtained.

Summers, too, can be filled with educational and recreational activities for young and old. Adult education classes, tours, trips, and recreational programs can be coordinated by the community school director. For youth, Flint includes such activities as the junior golf program, a boys' baseball program, the Flint Olympian and CANUSA (Canada-U.S.A.) Games, and the Mott camping program.

Appendix A at the conclusion of this chapter shows the daily community school programs from schools in two different communities to illustrate the variety of program options.

Financing

This section does not include a precise statement on how to finance a community school program. Some of the sources at the conclusion of this chapter and Chapter 2 will provide additional information of that nature. Obviously, the addition of educational programs will take increased financial support; however, reorganizing a traditional school into a community school can be accomplished with minimal initial increases. Hopefully, then, a successful community school program that better meets the needs of all taxpayers will receive additional financial support as it is required. Flint and other communities have found a significant increase in bond and millage approval after community school programs were initiated.

The Flint experience has shown that the added initial costs for a community school program are not high. An additional 6 to 8 percent is usually all that is required. Most of that increase goes to pay the community school director for administrative work above what he or she receives for teaching in the regular day program (they often teach fulltime in the afternoon) and for summer work. The adult education program often will pay for itself through participant fees, keeping the expense of increased programs quite low. Additional money required for custodial services, lighting, equipment, and miscellaneous is minimal.

Obtaining that initial 6 to 8 percent increase might not be an easy task. However, there are many sources that a community might examine. Foundations, various state and federal acts related to education or training, business and industry, community contributions, volunteer help, tuition and class fees, and money-making projects are to name a few. Those states currently appropriating money for community school programs and pending legislation in other states and at the federal level will greatly assist the community school movement.

Facilities

The facilities for education are very important to the community school program. Flint has found, for example, that a community room in each community school serves many purposes. It is a place where residents can meet together to discuss and plan for educational problems; it is a place for various community activities; and it is a place that citizens of the community can readily identify as their part of the school. When a community is just beginning to function under the community school concept, it probably can adapt one room in the school for such use. As the program and corresponding financial support grow, community school rooms can be constructed or enlarged.

Other facilities might already be available, but they need to be examined from a different viewpoint to consider new or expanded use for community school programs. The gymnasium, for example, can play an important role beyond typical physical education classes and athletics for youth. In Flint, special wheels and protective equipment are utilized so that students and parents can roller skate in the gyms. Gyms can also be utilized for scout troop activities, for adult recreational activities, and for large group meetings. In addition, libraries, auditoriums, playgrounds, and classrooms all might require expanded utilization.

Additional consideration on facilities centers upon their expanded use, time-wise and clientele-wise. Community schools can be open 16-24 hours each day, six or seven days a week, all year long. In addition, the schools are used as fully as possible by people of all ages and backgrounds. Consequently, air conditioning for certain parts of the country must be considered, especially for summer programs. Parking areas for adult education participants probably will need expansion. Finally, the comfort of the adult participant, especially the senior citizen, should be considered. This might require larger furniture for some rooms, coffee and smoking arrangements, and work tables or areas for some activities.

The discussion of facility arrangements thus far has dealt only with the school buildings or property. In the educative community, educational programs can be made available in many places. Thus, any plans to change existing school facilities should be coordinated with the potential use of existing community facilities. The YMCA might serve as a recreation center for after-school activities. Several churches might be sites for adult education classes. Each community probably will be able to develop a community school program utilizing various existing facilities.

UTILIZING THE COMMUNITY SCHOOL

Creating a community room for each school, hiring community school directors, and advertising several adult education classes will not automatically solve all community problems or even win additional financial support for education. The utilization of the community school concept for community betterment requires careful planning, coordination, and, especially, adaptation of the community school program to the particular community in which it is being implemented.

Initiating a community school program first requires some careful planning and analysis of the community's educational needs. This will involve such processes or actions as initiating community surveys, using committees for study and planning, and involving key community leaders in decision-making. Chapter 6 discusses in greater detail various community action processes and models.

Figure 2 displays how a community school program might be designed by utilizing various kinds of inputs to the planning process. Information from an assessment of community needs is one key input required. An evaluation of education already available in the school and in the community is also made. This evaluation process also becomes continual after the program begins, and is used as a constant feedback of information for future program-planning. A third major type of input comes from some type of community advisory committee charged with assisting in the developing of educational programs.

The community school director works in cooperation with other school personnel in designing educational activities based on the various inputs. The program is then administered by the director, his staff, and any other necessary persons. The success of the community school program will depend a great deal on the ability of the director to balance the program output and corresponding requirements on his time for administering the program with the inputs utilized in designing the programs and activities. The community school director must continually spend part of his time evaluating, working with advisory councils and assessing community needs.

Community advisory councils are important requirements to a successful community school program. The councils should be made up of representatives of all parts of community life. The purpose of councils is to involve parents and other residents in the development of educational programs for adults and youth in the community. Councils provide information on educational needs and interests, identify potential community leaders, give advice on educational programs, and work to improve cooperation and understanding between school personnel and community citizens.

The community citizen can also be used in many ways distinct from an advisory role. Assisting with programs for youth, helping to furnish the community room, and instructing some adult education courses are some of the ways lay citizens can be involved with the community school program. As was noted in the preceding chapter, involving the community resident in the decision-making for, planning toward, and implementation of, those programs affecting him or her will help to strengthen the community and assist in its adaptation to social change.

The final success of the community school in helping to meet various community needs rests on the cooperation and interaction

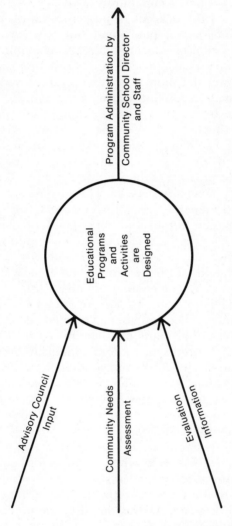

Figure 2. Designing the Community School Program

between people and agencies, both horizontally and vertically. This means that the community schools need to communicate how they can help in problem solution and community residents need to communicate how they would like the school to operate.

For a relatively small investment toward slightly altered facilities and a community school director, communities can receive expanded educational services aimed at bettering the lives of residents. The community school can become an agent of cohesiveness that brings the citizen, the neighborhood, and the larger community closer together and a center from which the educative community is developed. Some scholars even suggest that the community school is the last hope in solving the many problems threatening our very existence.

Much of this chapter has been written with the middle-sized, urban community as a model. That is because it all started in Flint, Michigan, and many of the principles and techniques were developed there. The community school concept has some limitations and it still is in a process of evolvement. But, the community school concept has had enough success that most communities should benefit by using it as a model around which to build an educative community.

Large communities such as New York City or Chicago will probably need to apply the concept on a neighborhood basis. Small or rural communities may need to develop community schools on a regional basis, where one community school director administers programs in several schools located in adjacent towns or areas. However applied, the community school concept has the potential of making education and the schools a greater tool in meeting the many needs of people.

APPENDIX A*

Schedule for a Rural Elementary Community School

TIME	ACTIVITY	ROOM	FREQUENCY
7-8 A.M.	Stay-in-shape program for men	Gym	Daily
8-8:30 A.M.	Spanish — grades 4-6	108	Daily
8:30-3 P.M.	Regular K-6 program	Various	Daily
10-11 A.M.	Prenatal nutrition for expectant mothers	Community Room	Weekly

*This material was adapted for use here from P. Keith Gregg, "A Community School: Day to Day Operations," in *The Role of the School in Community Education*, edited by Howard W. Hickey, Curtis Van Voorhees, and Associates (Midland, Michigan: Pendell Publishing Company, 1969), pp. 110-15.

TIME	ACTIVITY	ROOM	FREQUENCY
12-1 P.M.	Community businessmen's lunch	Community Room	Monthly
1:30-3 P.M.	Preparation of exotic Mexican foods	Community Room	Weekly
3-4 P.M.	Science enrichment grades 5 & 6	208	Twice weekly
3:30-5 P.M.	Boys' flagball — intramurals	Playground	Daily
3:30-5 P.M.	Girls' volleyball intramurals	Gym	Daily
5-7 P.M.	4-H club meeting	108	Monthly
7-10 P.M.	Adult education program: Silversmithing Basic reading Weaving Painting Farm Management	Various Rooms	Weekly
7-8 P.M.	Acrobatics & trampoline: Ages 7-10 (boys & girls)	Gym	Weekly
8-9 P.M.	Acrobatics & trampoline: Ages 11-14 (boys & girls)	Gym	Weekly
7-10 P.M.	Golden-agers historical society	210	Biweekly
7-9:30 P.M.	Teen-age music appreciation & dancing	Community Room	Weekly
7-8 A.M.	Jogging (Men and Women)	Playfield	Daily
7:30-8:30 A.M.	Sunrise singers — grades 4-6	108	Twice weekly
8:30-3 P.M.	Regular K-6 program	Various	Daily
10-11 A.M.	Prenatal & early childhood training for mothers	Community Room	Weekly
10-11 A.M.	Story hour for preschoolers	Library	Weekly
12-1 P.M.	Local businessmen's lunch with some students	Community Room	Weekly
1:30-3 P.M.	Soul food and its preparation	Community Room	Weekly
3-4 P.M.	Reading enrichment — grades 4-6	106 & 108	Twice weekly
3-4 P.M.	Girls' volleyball — intramurals	Gym	Daily
4-5 P.M.	Boys' basketball — intramurals	Gym	Daily
5-7 P.M.	Roller skating for families	Gym	Weekly

TIME	ACTIVITY	ROOM	FREQUENCY
7-10 P.M.	Adult education program: African history Painting Public speaking Drama Woodworking	Various Rooms	Weekly
7-9:30 P.M.	Teen dance	Community Room	Weekly
7-9 P.M.	Senior citizens' card-playing club	118	Weekly
7-10 P.M.	Committee to develop "black studies" program	116	Monthly
12-2 A.M.	Men's 2nd shift basketball league	Gym	Twice weekly

SELECTED BIBLIOGRAPHY

Books*

CAMPBELL, CLYDE M. *Toward Perfection in Learning.* Midland, Michigan: Pendell Publishing Company, 1969. 142 pages. Using a case history format, the editor has compiled several articles describing ways of working with educationally and culturally deprived youngsters. One chapter centers on the preparation of community school directors who will work in the inner city.

HENRY, NELSON B. (ed.). *The Community School.* Fifty-second Yearbook, Part II, National Society for the Study of Education. Chicago: University of Chicago Press, 1953. 292 pages. Index. The information is presented as a handbook for teachers and administrators in developing community school programs. It includes such topics as defining the community school, describing the program, outlining the organization and administrative needs, and describing how to help people, schools, and communities work together.

SHAW, NATHAN C. (ed.). *Administration of Continuing Education: A Guide for Administrators.* Washington, D.C.: National Association for Public School Adult Education, 1969. 438 pages. Index. Bibliography and selected readings. A compilation of chapters by various authors designed to serve as a guide to the public education of adults. Many chapters use the community school adult education program as a basis for examples and references. Major sections include "The Organization and Administration of Continuing Education," "Program Development and Operation," "The Adult Participant," "Improvement of Instruction," and "Research and Evaluation."

*See several books and periodicals cited in Chapter 2 for additional information.

WHITT, ROBERT L. *A Handbook for the Community School Director.* Midland, Michigan: Pendell Publishing Company, 1971, 133 pages. Bibliography. The author provides a concise handbook on the day-to-day problems facing a community school director. Chapters cover such topics as community involvement needs, obtaining program support, working with teachers, and developing a budget.

YOUNG, CLARENCE H., and QUINN, WILLIAM A. *Foundations for Living.* New York: McGraw-Hill Book Company, Inc., 1963. 254 pages. Index. This book portrays the life and story of C. S. Mott, founder of the Mott Foundation, and describes Flint, Michigan, the community in which he lives.

Films*

To Touch a Child — 16 mm — sound — color — 29 minutes. This film describes the community school program in Flint, Michigan, and illustrates how the community school concept can be adapted to other communities.

Thursday's Child — 16 mm — sound — color — 18½ minutes. This film portrays the community counselor role in the Flint community schools.

*The films are sponsored by the Mott Program of the Flint Board of Education, 923 E. Kearsley St., Flint, Michigan 48502.

CHAPTER 4

The Modern Family's Educational Needs

THE CHANGING FAMILY STRUCTURE

To say that the structure of the American family is changing might appear trite to some and sacrilegious to others. Change can be both threatening and lifesaving; yet, a society undergoing rapid and constant social change cannot expect its institutions to remain fixed. This chapter is based on the assumption that the family is changing and that its educational needs reflect this change.

Some authorities have predicted that radical changes will take place in the American family, or that it will disappear as we know it now. Communes, increasing divorce rates, and changing family roles are cited as evidence in support of these predictions. However, more than 90 percent of all Americans continue to live in family settings. As a matter of fact, the 1970 Census revealed a 10 percent rise in the number of families over the past decade. Thus, it is the contention here that the family as a basic institution will survive, but that it will also continue to change.

The transition of the United States from a rural to an urban society has initiated many of the changes in family functions. The farm family of yesterday was a tightly knit living unit, often comprised of parents and children as well as other relatives. All members contributed to the family's survival requirements. Roles were fixed, tasks were carried out according to age or status, and learning was based on traditional practices.

The roles of parents in the more traditional family have been described by Talcott Parsons, a sociologist. He identifies the father as an instrumental leader of the family. The instrumental role involves making the major family decisions and assuming the primary responsibility for child discipline and training. Parsons also described the mother as specializing in the expressive function. The expressive role involves responsibility for maintaining family solidarity and for the care and emotional support of children.

The urban family, however, has not evolved a standard set of traditional functions. Where mothers are employed outside the home, for example, children see their parents in different roles. Working women often take on subordinate instrumental roles, as they share in the responsibility for major family decision-making and money management. Fathers, too, can be seen in secondary roles. In families where fathers are concerned with, and spend time caring for, children, where they assist with tasks in the home, and where they share responsibility for child discipline, they begin to take on subordinate expressive roles. Various sources noted at the end of the chapter discuss in greater detail these evolving roles and their impact on family life.

The pressures of urbanization and change have put many strains on family living. Nearly one out of every four marriages, for example, ends in divorce; the rate is even higher in some states. This has led to a situation of short-term marriages and children growing up under several parents, for many of today's marriages involve previously married persons. The phenomena of divorce, remarriage, and the child with several parent figures in one lifetime have considerable impact on family life.

Another change affecting the family structure is a declining national birth rate. It remains to be seen whether this trend will continue, but the current ramifications are profound. Mothers, and fathers, too, are finishing the responsibilities of parenthood at earlier ages, freeing them for an increased pursuit of leisure activities. The diminished number of years in childbearing also has prompted many women to pursue careers, to obtain increased education, and to seek new roles within the home and the community, both before children are born and after they are reared. Finally, smaller families have tended to become more mobile, with fewer ties to any permanent conditions. This has created various kinds of problems that work to decrease family unity and stability.

An additional problem related to our changing times is the one-parent family. In addition to divorce and death resulting in one-parent families, our present economic system often has worked to cause them by driving the husband of the poor family from the home in search of work and/or so that the family unit can receive welfare monies. Various research has shown that single-parent home environments can result in serious problems for the children, especially in fatherless ones. Some of the consequences of fatherless homes include delinquent boys, people going through life seeking father figures, and a lifelong hate of men.

Rapid change itself is creating problems that affect individuals in various ways; one effect is emotionally maladjusted people who create tension and unhappiness in family settings because of their inability to cope with change. Maladjusted parents and unhappy marriages tend to create maladjusted and unhappy children, repeating a vicious cycle that is often unbreakable. Dealing with emotionally disturbed persons is a task for experts, but until these people are helped the families involved will suffer.

The adjustment to societal change probably will require some modifications in the family as we now know it. Margaret Mead, sociologist and anthropologist, has recommended a "two-step marriage" as one solution to some of the adjustment problems. The first step would include licensing a marriage, but the couple wouldn't have the right to bear children. Then, if the couple later decided that they wanted children, the second step would involve another licensed marriage with the privilege to have children included. Step two would be allowed only after a period of initial adjustment had expired for the couple, and, perhaps, after some form of mandatory parenthood education. Individual rights and freedoms will be issues requiring resolution before the two-step marriage or some comparable variation becomes a reality, but it could provide a way of dealing with some types of family problems resulting from rapid change.

In his interesting book, *Future Shock*, Alvin Toffler even predicts that some radically different schemes of family life will be attempted. For example, he suggests that the acceptance and training of parental professionals will be a reality of the future. These couples, who would be specially trained, licensed, professional parents, would be actual family units assigned to, and paid for, rearing children. The biological parents would accept a role resembling that of today's godparent.

Whether predictions of futurists regarding the family will come true or not is something we can only speculate about now and wait for time to give the answers. However, we do know that the structure of the family is in a current state of flux, a state initiated by the rural to urban transition and perpetuated by constant social change.

This situation has already given society the modern, streamlined family, a "nuclear" unit consisting of two parents and their small set of children. This kind of family structure actually was necessary to accommodate the requirements of industrialization and a technological society. It is suggested that this style of family, much more mobile than the traditional extended family of rural America, has become the major unit for child-rearing. How this form of family is affecting life and the educational process is not completely understood.

Figure 1 provides some understanding of the nuclear family's life cycle. Different stages in the cycle are recognizable, with the various child-rearing stages probably having the major importance for education and the schools. The educative community will need to be concerned with the needs of all people regardless of their stage in life, but the school's primary commitment currently is to school-age children.

The remainder of this chapter will deal with describing the family in relation to education and the schools. The discussion will center on family needs and how the school can help to meet these needs. The nuclear family described above will serve as a primary model of family life. Not all of the needs of the nuclear family, nor of the one-parent family, the experimental family, the poor family, or other types of families will be presented, but it is expected that the following information will provide some understanding of why the family, especially in the child-rearing years, must be considered in designing a program of community education.

THE FAMILY'S ROLE IN CHILD-REARING

For some time the family has been, and still is, the cornerstone of society. The family setting provides the child with his or her first look at life. The family teaches what is expected of people and what they can expect in life. The family also imparts the values that shape a person's beliefs, abilities, and actions. It is the belief of this author that the family will continue to be a major institution in American life and that every effort to strengthen the family unit must be made.

An environment of change has evolved the family into a nuclear unit: a unit that is small, mobile, and young. Although the modern family may have only one, two, or three children, each child has vital needs that must be met, especially if he or she is to be able to cope adequately with the increasing complexities of change. The family must help its members meet these needs as effectively as possible.

The family fulfills several obvious functions in caring for the child. Under normal conditions, food, shelter, and safety are the most basic functions provided by the home. Additional basic needs to be met include providing warmth, sleep, and physical cuddling, or, as it is sometimes referred to, "contact comfort."

Another function of the family is the intellectual development of children. The very early years of life are particularly crucial in the total span of human growth. This is when the child begins to acquire

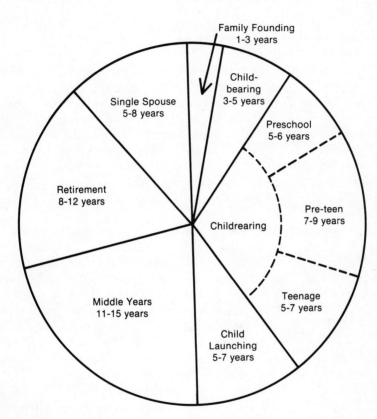

Figure 1. The Family Life Cycle

the ability to mentally process and use information. For example, researchers have discovered the following learning capabilities in infants:

> Three-week-old infants can learn to turn a lighted picture on and off by sucking on a special pacifier at a certain speed.
> Eight-week-old babies have learned to turn a mobile by pressing on a pillow.
> Very young babies will respond to speech sounds and can recognize human speech long before they utter their first word.

Thus, it is apparent that the first years, the first weeks, and even the first few hours after birth are extremely important parts of each person's life in an educational sense. The parents' responsibilities must include providing sensory and intellectual stimulation that will help each child reach his or her potential. The parents will also be a very important factor in developing a child's attitudes toward school and learning. Education can be a very powerful instrument for influencing the quality of a person's total life, but there must be continuity between what transpires in the home and what takes place in the school.

Another family function in child-rearing is the emotional development of the child. By the time a person begins school, his or her basic personality is formed. Thus, parents need to help children develop healthy feelings about themselves, a basic trust in life, and an understanding of the emotional impact one can have on his environment.

In addition to the basic functions fulfilled by parents, it is important that each home offers the child a setting of security. A feeling of security is necessary for intellectual development, for the development of a healthy self-image, for the creation of a personality that permits successful relationships with other people, and for the confidence to cope with the conditions of rapid change. It is difficult to establish a sense of security in a society of perpetual change and mobile families, but it is crucial that parents take the time and have the knowledge to establish a secure family setting.

Related to this situation of security is the phenomenon of the busy family, where individual family members often are so involved in their own activities that they don't really know one another. When children need parents for some reason, they usually want the help now, not always when it is convenient for the parent. Thus, there is a need for some form of unity within each family, where each member will be aware of, and respond to, the needs and feelings of others.

To be a unified family two basic ingredients must be present: love and affection. This means a father and mother showing affection toward the children as well as toward each other. It means the parents showing an interest in, and response to, their children's needs. It also means the children showing love for each other and for their parents. Several sources at the conclusion of the chapter discuss the importance of love and affection in the family.

The purpose of this section has been to show how very complex and important the role of the family is in preparing children for school and for life itself. The educational responsibility for a child is *critical, continuous,* and *demanding.* The school can and must play an important part in this responsibility for each child, but life in a family setting begins long before the school experiences are introduced. Thus, schools must work to strengthen the family by serving the needs of all family members before, during, and after formal schooling. Merging the community and the schools will require the treating of whole families as just that—families.

THE FAMILY AND THE SCHOOL

One assumption in the educative community is that one of the main purposes of the school is to serve all people in a variety of ways, and, by so doing, schools will also serve the larger society. However, the many current problems in our society are at least partial evidence that the school is not serving all people. The schools have not been very successful in involving parents in planning for education, in relating curriculum to family problems, and in developing problem-solving ability that can be used throughout a lifetime.

For example, when teachers present only subject-centered information and assume that the health and welfare of the child should be taken care of elsewhere, their very effectiveness as subject matter specialists can be lessened. The education of the child is influenced by the total environment in which he or she exists, including the home, the neighborhood, and the school. What is taught and how it is taught needs to be made relevant to everyday life.

Who, then, is involved in the educational process? In any community there are four main contributors: (1) the parents, (2) the community, (3) the child's peers, and (4) the schoolteachers. The purpose of the school in the educative community is to promote positive contributions by each.

As discussed earlier, parents initiate the educational process and support it throughout the child's first 16 or more years. In many ways the home is the most fundamental educational resource in the community, and parents are the most influential teachers. Parents teach values and attitudes; they teach their youngsters whether or whether not to like school; and they provide much of the out-of-school reinforcement of learning. Consequently, all relevant resources in the community should be geared to helping parents understand and undertake positive teaching roles.

The community has already been discussed in Chapter 2 as potentially a large contributor to child, parent, and citizen education. All possible community resources should be brought to bear on the learning process, both in and out of the school. School personnel will need to know how to utilize the educative community and parents will need to know what educational opportunities are available if they are to guide their children's educational use of the community.

A third contributor to the educational process is the child's peers. Learning to play is initiated in the home, but it is certainly reinforced by peer-group relationships. Social relationships, conversational styles, and personal grooming and clothing habits are also learned and determined through peer-group contacts. Thus, parents and teachers both need to recognize the importance of the peer group and use the potential of such relationships to benefit the educational process.

Schoolteachers, of course, have a fundamental role in the educational process. However, the teaching of subject matter must be balanced with an understanding of how to relate the class content to the reality of the family, community, and world environments. This requires caring about families and reinforcing in school the values taught in the home rather than imposing some value system that is thought to be better. This is perhaps most crucial at the elementary school level, when the initial transition from home to school takes place.

The school's responsibility to the family is varied and complex; it goes far beyond the fundamental teaching role. The parents, for example, need to be aware of and involved in curriculum planning, as the curriculum used in schools can cycle back to affect the family. This is illustrated where a minority-group child fails to ever see himself or herself represented in the textbooks being utilized and becomes confused or feels insecure. Correcting this includes not only the utilization of text material that is family oriented, but also the use of examples, learning exercises, and out-of-class activities related to the family and community living situations and needs. Such activities as developing parent clubs, involving parents in curriculum-planning committees, and introducing parents to community and family educational opportunities are additional ways the school can contribute to the family.

Another responsibility of the school should be to learn as much as possible about each child before he or she starts school, so that education can be designed to meet particular needs. Children coming to school hungry or emotionally upset, for example, can't be expected to participate very actively or successfully in the educational process. This means that teachers, counselors, community school directors, and principals should visit homes regularly to understand the needs and potential of preschool youngsters and to help families understand how they can support the educational process. Visiting the homes should continue after children start school, to help meet problems in school that result from the home life, to help parents in their educational efforts with children, and to help children understand how they may contribute to the family and community life.

In addition to the usual curriculum that helps to prepare students for living, schools need to help children and youth to better understand the dynamics of living in a family setting. This has usually involved the introduction into school systems of courses centered on education for family living. Unfortunately, the curriculum has often been tagged or developed as sex education, rather than as family living as a whole; the resulting programs have usually been short-lived or inadequate. In the schools where a family life curriculum has become a regular part of the total curriculum, most teachers, parents, and students have been enthusiastic in their support. Hopefully, the future will find additional schools adding successful family life courses from early elementary through high school.

The relationship between the family and the school is complex. Many forces contribute to the teaching-learning process, including those both inside and outside of the school. Thus, as we think of the educative community concept developed in earlier chapters, the school must be maintained and strengthened in its role as a developer of human resources.

THE NATURE OF THE SCHOOL IN FAMILY AND COMMUNITY PROBLEM-SOLVING

Chapter 3 discussed the potential of the community school as a center for education directed toward improving the entire community.

Where communities have implemented the community school concept, it is assumed that developing and enhancing the problem-solving
skills of community residents will be one important objective. However, communities that do not have community schools still require
community residents and school personnel with problem-solving
abilities. This section will present some ideas and information that
should reveal to all schools and community citizens the nature of the
school in solving various family and community problems.

The total family and the community need the problem-solving
expertise of the school, as does the child. In communities throughout
America, the idea of education for responsible living is drawing together parents, school personnel, and various other representatives
from community life. The thought is that training for successful roles
in families and in society can be made more systematic and widespread.

Educational programs designed as parent education have had
considerable success in some parts of the United States. Usually offered as adult education, courses on child-rearing, sexuality, inter-
personal relationships, self-understanding, and human growth and
development have had a large number of participants. For example, in
a recent year more than 22,000 adults enrolled in parent education
classes in the Los Angeles public schools. However, much more can
be accomplished in most communities.

Helping parents understand more fully their educational roles in
the lives of children is one of the educational tasks that all schools
could undertake. For example, many parents require some training to
understand how they can and should reinforce the educational process. Thus, through some form of adult education parents could learn
how to stimulate the physical and social development of their children
by providing an enriched environment from birth through the first
several years. Several references at the end of the chapter give additional guidance on this subject.

There are also many parents requiring help because they have
children with special problems. Parents of the handicapped (physically, mentally, and emotionally) usually require assistance on how
they can provide their children with special attention and training.
Additional problem categories requiring special assistance from the
schools include such families as those with delinquent children, the
single-parent family, and the unmarried mother.

Federal monies are being invested in schools for purposes of
promoting positive family and community life. Various programs and
acts provide a variety of training programs in needed areas. Perhaps

the most widely known program is Operation Headstart. It was initiated in 1965 as a supplemental summer experience for preschool children. The summer experience was not found to be extensive enough, so it has been refined in scope since then to include school activities for a full year. In addition, there are now opportunities for parents to improve their own self-image, to assist in the program as aides or family assistants, and to become involved in policy decision-making.

The Department of Health, Education, and Welfare has also implemented some parent-child centers in various communities. Working in conjunction with the schools, the centers are designed to promote communications between parents and to help them become aware of what is available of an educational or problem-solving nature in the community and in the schools. Some centers even provide assistance in the homes on particular problems.

A growing need throughout the country is for day care centers. In more and more families both parents are employed; consequently, some form of daily child care is required if they have preschool children. It is proposed that school systems could provide the major assistance for this particular situation. Perhaps an earlier contact with the child would even allow schools to have a greater impact on learning abilities and achievements as a result of educational continuity and positive attitudes toward learning being developed.

The philosophy that must accompany the total contact with the child and the involvement of parents or other citizens is that education is lifelong, continuous, and encompassing both in and out of school activities. Thus, the impact of education upon the solution of social problems will depend on developing appropriate leadership skills and attitudes that promote problem-solving and decision-making abilities.

For example, these attitudes and leadership skills could be utilized in the reduction of poverty. Opportunities for educational improvement should be the basic attack on poverty. Schools can offer programs and leadership in assisting people to engage in their own improvement. Many families can be reached only through one-to-one contacts, but the school, especially the community school, has much to offer. Classes on such topics as budgeting, home repair and maintenance, food buymanship and preparation, and clothing maintenance could provide additional survival skills. Home visits by school officials could also provide a solution to some individual problems.

Children must learn, must know how to learn, and must be able to learn continually throughout their lives if they are to cope successfully with the many changing demands of living in a complex world.

Thus, learning opportunities provided by schools to youth and adults could be developed around the stages of the human life cycle, around contemporary social issues, and around the promotion of future-relevant behavioral skills. The ability to adapt to change is a much needed skill in our society; schools must help people acquire this skill.

The restoration of education to community life is a theme supported throughout this book. A community-centered educational program can help people adapt to change and to learn to solve their own problems. It also may even contribute to the cohesiveness of the family, an important factor during a time when increasing vertical relationships are tending to pull apart communities, families, and their associations with the schools.

Thus, it seems imperative that schools and families work together on various needs. This means that teachers strive to know and understand their community. It also means that parents become involved with planning and implementing school programs. The school becomes a rallying point where families and communities find answers to questions and acquire the strength to solve various problems. Perhaps the community school described in Chapter 3 can even come to be known as the family-community school, where both family and community problems would be the focal point for curriculum planning and where the coordination of various community programs would begin.

SOME DEFINITIONS

Expressive Parental Role — This role involves responsibility for maintaining family solidarity, for controlling family tensions, and for providing the care and emotional support of children. The mother traditionally has occupied this role.

Expressive-Subordinate Role — In the modern family an increasing number of fathers are beginning to participate in and provide secondary support to the expressive role. This is usually in the form of assisting with various household responsibilities, assuming a larger role in child-rearing, and more openly showing expression of affection toward the wife and children.

Family — A group of persons related by blood or marriage who occupy a common residence. The main functions of the family are childbirth, child-rearing, and social discipline of its members.

Instrumental Parental Role — This role involves the responsibility for interpreting the outside world to the family, the solution of family problems, the management of daily family needs, and the discipline and training of children. The father traditionally has occupied this role.

Instrumental-Subordinate Role—In the modern family where mothers are increasingly occupying paid jobs outside the home, they are beginning to occupy this role. This usually entails a sharing of responsibility for money management and decision-making.

Nuclear Family—A family unit made up of father, mother, and children and having weaker ties with the extended network of relatives than previously existed. However, ties are maintained somewhat through letters, phone calls, and periodic visits.

Peer Group—A group of agemates, usually in the form of an adolescent group or gang.

SELECTED BIBLIOGRAPHY

Books

DODSON, FITZHUGH. *How to Parent.* Los Angeles: Nash Publishing, 1970. 442 pages. Appendixes. A variety of useful information for parents is presented—and it is written with the average parent as the audience. The first half of the book takes the child from infancy through preschool, describing basic behaviors, needs, and learning potentials. The second half discusses various topics concerning the child's growth and development. An additional asset of the book is the inclusion of several appendixes on such topics as toys, books, and children's records, with recommendations for their educational usage.

DREIKURS, RUDOLF. *The Challenge of Parenthood.* New York: Meredith Press, 1958. 334 pages. Index. The author provides advice on specific situations and promotes a basic attitude of mind and heart toward children and child training. The reasons behind children's behavior are explored. The methods of training, common mistakes in child-rearing, and understanding the child are some of the topics included.

DUVALL, EVELYN M. *Family Development.* 4th Edition. Philadelphia: Lippincott Company, 1971. 520 pages. Index. Glossary of terms. The author discusses the regularities of family change over the life cycle. Eight stages of the family life cycle are presented and supported by various data. Charts and graphs illustrate the information.

GINOTT, HAIM G. *Between Parent and Child.* New York: The Macmillan Company, 1965. 223 pages. Index. Bibliography. Appendix. This book offers suggestions for dealing with the daily situations and problems faced by parents of children from infancy through pre-teen years. There is advice on discipline, sex education, children's fears, and situations calling for professional help. The theme of the book deals with the premise that mutual respect and dignity between parent and child are needed and possible.

_____. *Between Parent and Teenager.* New York: The Macmillan Company, 1969. 255 pages. Index. Bibliography. This is a follow-up to the author's first book listed above. Such topics as rebellion, anger, praise, relationships, and drugs are covered.

GLASSER, PAUL H., and GLASSER, LOIS N. (eds.). *Families in Crisis.* New York: Harper & Row, 1970. 405 pages. Index. This is a book of readings on three major areas of family crisis: Poverty, disorganization, and physical and mental illness. The essays by various authors present intellectual and emotional insights into the three crisis areas. Various problem aspects and suggested solutions are included.

LEMASTERS, E. E. *Parents in Modern America.* Homewood, Illinois: The Dorsey Press, 1970. 232 pages. Index. Written in realistic and lively terms, this book offers a critical review of the various literature on parent-child relationships and suggests that the literature has not usually approached parenthood from the parent's point of view; books have tended to be child-centered. Chapters are included on the societal setting of parenthood, folklore about parenthood, changes in parent roles, and a special analysis of parents by various categories. The final chapter presents and discusses some interesting parental models.

MEDINNUS, GENE R., and JOHNSON, RONALD C. (eds.). *Child and Adolescent Psychology.* New York: John Wiley & Sons, Inc., 1970. 662 pages. Author index. This book contains a variety of articles contributed by many authors. Topics included are "Methods in Child Psychology," "Basic Factors in Development," "The Family and Its Influence on Development," "Societal Influences on Socialization," "The End Product," and "Adolescence."

MICHAEL, DONALD N. *The Next Generation: The Prospects Ahead for the Youth of Today and Tomorrow.* New York: Random House, Inc., 1965. 207 pages. Index. Appendixes. This book examines various trends in the American society in an attempt to analyze where they are heading. Such topics as the economy, technology, marriage and the family, education, and leisure are examined. The author urges that we explore more honestly and intently what values and goals we want inculcated into our youth.

RODMAN, HYMAN (ed.). *Marriage, Family, and Society.* New York: Random House, 1965. 302 pages. Index. Appendix. Presented as a reader on marriage and the family, this book is written from a sociological view. Various authors discuss such topics as dating, mate selection, husband-and-wife relations, parent-and-child relations, and the changing American family. The final chapter discusses Talcott Parsons' view of the changing family.

SUSSMAN, MARVIN B. *Sourcebook in Marriage and the Family.* Third Edition. Boston: Houghton Mifflin Company, 1968. 594 pages. Index. Name index. Biographical notes. This sourcebook contains 75 articles on such topics as birth, marriage, social class, family structure, and family problems. The book also includes a section on the trends in family research and theory and concludes with a discussion of prospects for the American family.

Periodicals

The Family Coordinator. Published quarterly by the National Council on
   Family Relations, Minneapolis, Minnesota. The journal presents various
   articles on education, counseling, and service as they relate to the family.
Journal of Marriage and the Family. Published quarterly by the National
   Council on Family Relations, Minneapolis, Minnesota. The journal primarily presents research articles on various family-living topics. An inter-
   national section and book reviews are included in each issue.
Parents' Magazine. Published monthly by The Parents' Institute, a division
   of Parents' Enterprise, Inc., New York. The magazine includes articles
   on various aspects of child and parent relationships, family health, and
   family fun.
Psychology Today. Published monthly by Communications/Research/Ma-
   chines, Inc., Carmel Valley Road, Del Mar, California. The magazine
   centers its articles on psychology, society, and human behavior. Articles
   on the child are frequently included.

CHAPTER 5

Community Coordination and Cooperation

THE NEED FOR COORDINATION AND COOPERATION

Central to the concept of the educative community is that the school and the community must cooperate with each other. Activating the community into a living learning laboratory is not possible without close coordination and cooperation. This is true for all types of communities, but particularly so in large, urban communities, where the interaction of people with each other and with organizations is complex and ever-changing.

Coordinated community programs and planning efforts are necessary to stimulate both educational and economic development. This means that problem-solving is carried out by people cooperating with each other. It also means that decisions affecting a community are made by a representative body of leaders and that information regarding decisions is communicated throughout the community.

The above two paragraphs represent an ideal situation. Unfortunately, efforts in cooperation and in the coordination of programs are less than ideal in many communities. The horizontal relationships and linkages between organizations and between people are weak or not maintained. For example, governmental officials pass laws that affect the schools without adequate consultation with school officials. Business and industry develop various goods and services but do not consider the ecological ramifications. Educators work on developing various curricula for children, but they fail to incorporate unique community resources and characteristics into the educational programs.

An actual example of what can result from the lack of close coordination and cooperation comes from a large Michigan community. A large electrical industry had a critical need for secretaries and clerical help but virtually no additional need for electricians or electronic technicians. However, the community's technical and community college was graduating large numbers of people trained in the electrical fields but only a few secretarial and clerically trained people. The absence of horizontal relationships prevented these two agencies from coordinating needs with existing resources.

If communities would carefully and continually coordinate the planning on various aspects of community living, there is a potential for many benefits. Coordinated and long-range planning could allow agencies and organizations to develop varied educational programs with existing facilities and resources. As an illustration, the YMCA and its supporters might decide that constructing a new recreational facility was unnecessary if it was found that the community college already had similar facilities under construction. Or, as in the above example, a closer coordination of programs and needs between the industry and the community college might have resulted in a higher community employment rate and a lower out-migration of skilled people seeking jobs elsewhere.

Small communities, too, could benefit from cooperation with other communities. Combined fire and police protection, joint health planning, and coordinated construction of recreation facilities are some of the possible cooperative ventures. An existing effort at coordination increasingly being accomplished in rural areas is the consolidation of school districts. This has become a necessity in many parts of the country because of the rising costs of education and a decreasing population base.

There are many more illustrations of the benefits that can be realized through community cooperation and coordination. The references at the conclusion of this chapter include some of the illustrations. Appendixes A and B provide a description of two current attempts to promote community cooperation and coordination.

COORDINATING EDUCATIONAL PROGRAMS

There are many agencies and organizations in each community that provide programs and services of an actual or potential educational nature. To realize the benefits of mutual planning and coordination, the common concerns of these agencies or groups need to be recognized. The following is an identification of some common concerns found in communities:

COMMON CONCERNS	SOME INVOLVED AGENCIES AND ORGANIZATIONS
Intellectual and creative growth	Schools, churches, libraries, museums, art galleries, community colleges, and youth organizations
Physical education and fitness	Schools, YMCA, and YWCA
Health education	Schools, doctors, dentists, hospitals, and health associations
Recreation and leisure	Schools, YMCA, YWCA, City Recreation Department, senior citizen groups, and private groups
Retirement and pre-retirement	Senior citizen groups, business and industry, and retirement homes
Employment and career education	Schools, business and industry, community colleges, and employment agencies

Communities need to recognize these various commonalities and build on them through their program-planning, facility construction, and program implementation. Spending that scarce dollar for educational programs always needs careful consideration and coordination.

Figure 1 provides an illustration of how a community could plan for and coordinate some educational programs by building on the common concerns of several agencies. One of the concerns of the school is career education. As depicted in the figure, this concern is also common to the local business agency and the state employment agency. Common concern A might be the desire to provide an on-the-job exploration of certain careers. In this case Agency 1 could provide the students, Agency 2 the experience, and Agency 3 the coordination of the exploration experiences.

Those concerns more common to only two of the agencies also could be important. Common concern B might be a representative of the local business coming to the school to coordinate a discussion of employment opportunities in his area of expertise. Concern C might be the school counselor providing some test scores and information on graduated students to the state agency. Common concern D might include the state agency sending prospective employees to the business for job interviews.

Communication among various community agencies and the schools is important if educational programs are to be coordinated. This is to prevent a conflict in educational goals. For example, if the school system is preparing students primarily to enter four-year colleges that exist outside the community but local industries feel that the schools should be preparing students for employment within the

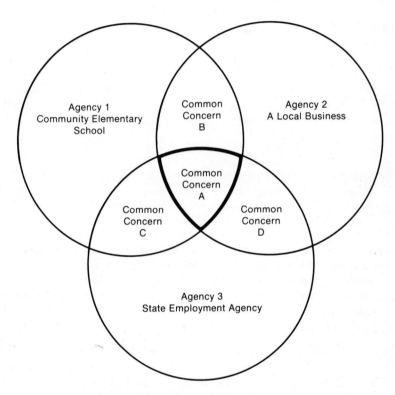

Figure 1. The Commonalities of Three Community Agencies

community, there can be conflict, confusion, and lack of support for what the schools are doing. How to build communication patterns will be discussed in the next section of this chapter.

The educational system can no longer remain autonomous and separate from the rest of the community. Nor can various agencies and organizations providing educational services afford programs that will meet all community needs. Consequently, there is a need for some central coordination of the educational programming carried out by the schools and other agencies if maximum service to each community is to be provided.

The author recently studied several American communities and found some facts that verify the critical need for a centralized coordination of educational programs. For example, in one community the following agencies or groups were carrying out educational programs that dealt with Nutrition Education:

Public Schools — Home economics classes on nutrition and food preparation for teenage girls
Community Action Program — Nutrition information and referrals
County Welfare Office — Food stamps and commodity food distribution
Cooperative Extension Service — Expanded Nutrition Program (Federally supported program) paraprofessional aides who visited homes and presented nutrition information
State Health Association — Nutrition education literature
Head Start Program — Nutrition education for children and parents
Catholic Social Services — Emergency food distribution and nutrition literature

There is obvious overlap of effort and resources in situations such as the one described above, and, in this specific situation, it was found that some families were being contacted by several agencies for purposes of providing nutrition education and information. The central coordination of educational programs might have prevented the overlap.

The duplication of educational efforts in communities must be eliminated if there is to be a chance of meeting the many needs of residents. The many concerns of organizations should be determined and this information communicated throughout the community so that agencies can work together according to both the strengths and weaknesses of each. Thus, it is suggested that the central coordination of their educational programs should provide for a greater return to the total community dollars invested. A later section discusses the concept of central coordination in greater detail.

BUILDING COMMUNICATION PATTERNS

Communication is a cornerstone to cooperation and coordination. The strength of horizontal community relationships depends on the type and amount of communications carried out between agencies and people. Thus, there is a need for a good communication network in each community. The network must encompass the entire community, and, for purposes of building the educative community, is especially important between the school and community residents. The school needs to inform the community as to what it is doing, and community agencies and residents need to tell school officials what is needed or how the community can help the schools be more efficient in their educational efforts.

Communication is defined as the process of passing information and understanding from one person to another. Figure 2 displays the communications process as it would operate at a community level. For example, the school superintendent determines that a report on the past school year's music program should be given to community residents. The administrative staff then develops a two-page report. They decide that the local newspaper should be the channel of communication and the report is published in the Sunday edition. Interested parents read the report and interpret it according to their children's needs and interests. Feedback is supplied in the form of letters of support to the superintendent and by a large number of children becoming involved in the music program for the first time.

This rather simple illustration does not include all aspects of a good communication network. Good communication needs to be planned and continuous. This means that if the network of communication breaks down anywhere in the community, or if thorough communication efforts are not made on a regular basis, then some segment of the population could be excluded. In the above example, those parents and citizens who did not receive the Sunday paper might never hear about the music program and could therefore fail to provide additional support for the program.

Good communication systems must also be flexible. Flexible communication is based on the utilization of different channels of communication to reach different audiences for each cause. The parent of the elementary child might be reached through a letter sent home with the child and through the local PTA organization. The Head Start parent is reached through a personal contact by a program aide and through the newspaper. The senior citizen is reached through the senior citizen organization or by phone. The potential

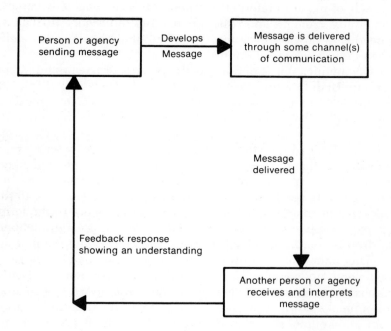

Figure 2. The Communications Process

adult education participant is reached through a newspaper advertisement or through literature distributed at his or her place of employment.

People are bombarded daily with numerous communication attempts. Radio, television, newspapers, billboards, and mail are all communication channels utilized intensively. Thus, the communication efforts by schools must be concise and accurate: accurate to build confidence on the part of the people receiving the messages and concise to compete successfully with all the other communicative efforts.

It seems clear that if a school system is to effectively serve the community from which support is solicited, there are several communication objectives that need to be fulfilled:

1. Accurate information about the schools must be provided.
2. Accurate information about the community and its resources must be obtained.
3. Information about new trends and developments in education must be provided.
4. A feeling of shared concern and responsibility about the school needs to be developed.
5. The importance of education to the community needs to be promoted.

Smaller schools can usually meet these objectives through the direction of the school superintendent and cooperation by other school personnel. Larger school systems often require the efforts of one or more persons involved solely with communication between the schools and the community. Whatever the effort required, the development of a good communication network is crucial to successful cooperation and coordination and to developing linkages between school, family, and community.

ESTABLISHING A CENTRAL COORDINATING AGENCY

Coordinating the various educational efforts in a community and promoting the cooperation necessary to activate the educative community is no easy task. Many communities have attempted to provide some coordination of various planning efforts through community, county, or regional planning boards. However, these coordinating agencies usually have been concerned with planning related to economic growth and seldom have dealt with education. To date, very few American communities have tried to provide some centralized coordination of their various educational programs and activities.

Consequently, it is suggested that one educational organization in each community should be designated or created as a central co-ordinating agency. Three agencies that might perform such roles are the following: (1) community or public schools, (2) community colleges, or (3) agencies that would be newly created or legislated for the job. Each of these agencies will be described and a rationale will be included to support their undertaking such tasks. Those communities desiring to have a central coordinating body could pick the agency best fitting their particular situation or could select some other agency existing in their community.

There are many advantages in selecting the community or public school as the central coordinating agency. In locations where the community school concept is in force, community elementary schools are found in almost every neighborhood. Public schools, too, are located in every community or in most large community neighborhoods. This provides the advantage of ready access to, and acquaintance with, most residents. Passage of the national legislation to promote community schools that was discussed in Chapter 3 could increase this advantage throughout American communities.

The community or public school is already the center of K-12 programs and many other educational activities in those communities where the concept of the community school or the educative community is in force. It would not take much additional effort and expense for community schools to act as a communication channel for information on educational opportunities and needs. Such services as referring people to those educational opportunities best fitting their needs and keeping account of skilled workers or skilled worker needs could be performed. Regular public schools could also undertake such tasks, but additional resources and a greater emphasis on community involvement would be required.

The community college, a two-year institution of higher and continuing education, is another agency that potentially could provide the needed coordination in some American communities. Community college staffs usually contain many educators with coordinating skills and experiences. In addition, most community colleges are making an increased commitment to providing community services and educational programs off the central campus. Successfully implementing these programs will require cooperation with and from other educational institutions; consequently, community colleges might be able to expand their cooperative efforts and provide community-wide coordination.

Community colleges do not exist in every community. However, additional colleges are being constructed in many communities. Thus, an increasing number of community leaders will have this institution as one of the agencies to choose from. In addition, the community college will undoubtedly play an important supportive role in many localities even if community or public schools are designated as central coordinating agencies.

There are several reasons why an entirely new agency might function successfully in a central coordinating role. For example, there would not be the need to incorporate new roles and personnel into an existing organization, as people would be employed when they are needed to fill actual or evolving roles. In addition, a new agency would not have strong vertical relationships to agencies or concerns outside of its community and could concentrate all its resources and efforts on promoting communication and coordination. Accepting the total community, rather than some specific clientele, as its constituency might also provide a similar advantage.

The proposal put forth in this section for expanding the roles of the community school, public school, and community college or for creating a new agency to serve as a central coordinating agency will require some additional resources and personnel. Expanded communication facilities, computer services, and personnel trained as educational planners or change specialists are some of the potential requirements. The proposed suggestion needs additional research and study to determine all of the changes that will be required before an agency can assume a central coordinating role. However, the duplication of effort and large expense of education that exist in most communities make imperative the consideration of some means to promote better cooperation and coordination.

FUNCTIONS OF A CENTRAL COORDINATING AGENCY

The functions that a central coordinating agency could undertake are many and varied. They also give some clues to the personnel and resources that would be required for the coordinating role. The following discussion on functions is based on the assumption that each community would designate that organization best suited for the coordinating task.

One of the basic functions that a coordinating agency could undertake has already been mentioned. Such an agency could be the central core of communication channels for the various community agencies and organizations involved with community and educational programs. Figure 3 shows how various communications might flow through the agency. A school is used for illustration, but any other agency might be utilized. For example, occupational information, information on educational opportunities, and other community information could be solicited by or sent to the elementary school of a local neighborhood. This information would then be available in one central location and also would be sent to the other schools in the larger community for an expanded availability. If it is a small or rural community, one central school in the community or even in the county might be designated for the communication role.

Related to the communication function is that of a central referral service. Information on job opportunities, educational and training opportunities, recreational opportunities, and even some counseling services connected to the referral information could be provided to people as they require it. In the figure, one example illustrated includes referring people to various jobs or cooperating with local employment agencies. The central agency might be able to identify the educational training required and available for entrance into certain occupations. Appendix C at the conclusion of this chapter displays a listing of possible community programs or agencies to be considered in a referral program.

Another function for the coordinating body could be to act as an information collection unit and clearinghouse on educational programs, opportunities, and resources. This would encompass the collection of all information useful in educational planning. The sharing of community information among residents, agencies, and organizations and the continual assessment of the extent of various educational investments according to the community needs could be a part of the clearinghouse function. It might also include keeping a current inventory on the level of human resource development. This information and an analysis of current training programs then could be given to local educational organizations for their use in planning future educational programs. Extensive use of modern computers would facilitate such a function.

A central agency could fulfill a vital function in coordinating the involvement of local citizens and community leaders in planning and decision-making for education. As Figure 3 shows, the school might send a representative to the planning sessions of various community agencies and organizations for purposes of supplying information and promoting coordinated efforts. The coordinating agency could also compile information on the skills and abilities of community residents and suggest to the various educational organizations the names of people who might supply a particular kind of assistance.

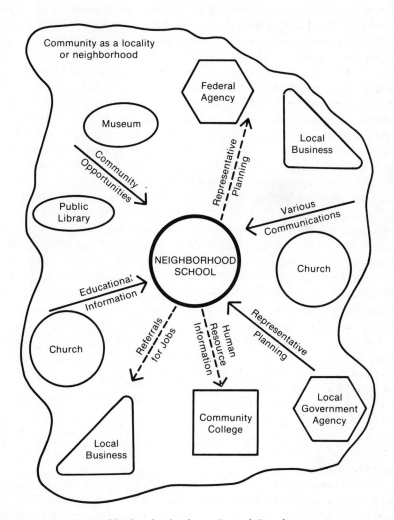

Figure 3. Neighborhood School as a Central Coordinating Agency

A final function for the coordinating agency to be described here is that of evaluation. The coordinating agency could implement a periodic evaluation of the various educational programs available in the community. This would provide feedback information to help improve the educational efforts of community organizations and would help to determine where additional or different programs were needed.

The potential of coordinating education through a central agency seems great, especially if many communities across the country would implement the proposed concept. Educational planning specialists could be trained to work in such coordinating agencies. Information on successful programs also could be shared between communities. Furthermore, if the community or public school assumes the coordinating role, a greater utilization of existing facilities and expertise in American communities might be realized.

Investing in education is a necessary requirement for community and human growth. It is also an expensive and complicated venture. The prevention of overlap, confusion, and conflict is necessary to obtain the largest benefit from that scarce investment dollar. A greater cooperation among community residents and agencies and a better coordination of educational programs will contribute to these requirements. A central coordinating agency in each community should facilitate this contribution.

APPENDIX A

PROJECT COMMUNI-LINK
An Approach to Community-Wide Educational Programming

Project COMMUNI-LINK is a federally funded, multi-state attempt to facilitate communication and resource utilization for basic educational programming in rural communities. The project is designed to demonstrate that adults in rural areas who lack opportunity, or who are not motivated, to participate in educational programs will do so when programs to satisfy their economic and social needs are made available to them.

The project is based on the assumption that a person is a complex behavioral organism having many needs which require satisfaction in a variety of ways. For various reasons (such as time or resource constraints, administrative policies, and differing views on the purpose of educational programs) attempts to meet these varied needs often achieve only minimal success. The project proposes that a comprehensive approach to community-wide programming and a coordinated approach by state and community agencies will overcome the various barriers to greater success.

The attainment of the goals described above will be attempted in two ways:

1. Professionals, paraprofessionals, and volunteer organization leaders on state and local levels who are involved in rural community educational programs will receive assistance and training in developing more effective communication linkages in their respective communities.
2. Consultation and demonstrations will be provided to community leaders who are concerned with the motivation, recruitment, and teaching of disadvantaged and other adults.

Various activities and techniques are being utilized to develop additional skills in community residents and to provide a closer linkage between community agencies:

1. Community leaders are being trained in decision-making through a simulated gaming device.
2. Community adult education councils are being formed.
3. The elimination of competitive programs is being attempted.
4. The compilation and distribution of community directories containing the names and descriptions of agencies and organizations is being carried out.

Nineteen states currently are involved with the project. Colorado State University, Fort Collins, Colorado, provides the primary staff support and leadership.

APPENDIX B

Senior Information and Referral Service:
A Project for Community-Wide Information and Referral

In Westchester County, New York, the Council of Social Agencies is serving older people in the county through a central clearinghouse of information on available services. The project also has developed a referral service to help people contact the agency or organization in the county best suited to provide a particular service or activity.

The clearinghouse, a centralized "Senior Information and Referral Service" (SIRS), has a staff that locates, identifies, and publicizes existing county services. The staff also provides counseling when it is required and directs the referral service. A trunk-line telephone system is utilized so that calls can be made from any part of the county for the cost of a local call.

APPENDIX C

Community Referral:
Organizations or Activities Common to Many Communities

Adult Basic Education
Adult Education Program
Alcoholism Counseling
Association for Retarded Children
Boy Scout Council
Career Development Organization
Chamber of Commerce
Child Guidance Clinic
Churches (various)
City Housing Administration
City Planning Administrator
Community Action Program
Community College
Community Mission House
Cooperative Extension Service
Council of Churches
County Medical Associations
County Planning Commission
County Welfare Agency
Department of Vocational Rehabilitation
Emergency Food and Medical Services
Employment Agency (state)
Family Planning
Family Service Association
Girl Scout Council
Good Neighbor Community Services
Goodwill Industries
Head Start
Home and Neighborhood Development
Human Rights Commission
Indian Center
League of Women Voters
Legal Services
Medical and Dental Clinics
Mental Health Association
Neighborhood Youth Corps
Parochial Schools
Parochial Social Services
Personal Crisis Service
Psychiatric Clinic
Public Schools (Community Schools)

Salvation Army
Senior Citizen Organization
Service Organizations (various)
United Services
Veterans Service Center
VISTA (Volunteers in Service to America)
Vocational Rehabilitation Service
Volunteers of America
YMCA (Young Men's Christian Association)
YWCA (Young Women's Christian Association)

SOME DEFINITIONS

Communication Process—A process through which explanations, ideas, information, directions, feelings, and attitudes are passed from one person to another. Communications may be oral, written, or implied. They may utilize symbols and various channels for message development and transmission.

Community College—A two-year educational institution that provides technical and vocational education, college transfer programs, noncredit education, and community service programs.

SELECTED BIBLIOGRAPHY

GRIFFITHS, DANIEL E., et al. Organizing Schools for Effective Education. Danville, Illinois: Interstate Printers & Publishers, Inc., 1962. 338 pages. Index. Selected bibliography. Centering on the administrative and organizational needs of a school system, the authors describe how a school can be designed to best serve the community and society. Job descriptions of administrative positions and several case studies of school districts are provided.

PAUL, BENJAMIN D. (ed.). Health, Culture and Community: Case Studies of Public Reactions to Health Programs. New York: Russell Sage Foundation, 1955. 493 pages. Index. The book presents the case studies of several successes and failures in health programming at the community level. Some understanding of the complexities and benefits in coordinating various community efforts is provided.

SCHRAMM, WILBUR (ed.). The Processes and Efforts of Mass Communication. Urbana, Illinois: University of Illinois Press, 1954. 586 pages. Indexes of subjects and names. Further reading. This book is a collection of articles describing how the communication process works. The reader should find some application toward building good communications between school and community.

Additional references can be found in the following sources referenced in earlier chapters:

Chapter 1: Biddle
          Sanders
          Warren
Chapter 2: Hickey
          Sumption
          Totten

CHAPTER 6

Processes for Community Change

ANALYZING COMMUNITY PROBLEMS

Solving the various problems of our society and of our communities is not an easy task. We have suggested in earlier chapters that education can be used to facilitate finding some of the solutions. Community education has been described as a means by which the problems of people are central to the design of education. The activation of the educative community is an attempt to help people learn how to live more satisfying lives. Yet, this cannot be accomplished without first analyzing community problems and needs and then developing educational and community programs that will meet needs or provide solutions to problems.

This chapter will provide a brief discussion of various strategies, processes, and models for problem-solving available to communities. Whether administered by the public school or some other agency, successful community change through education will require systematic analysis and planning. The processes used successfully in one community might not transfer directly to another community. Thus, each unique community should be able to choose one or more approaches that apply appropriately to its particular situation.

There are many requirements to be met in effective problem-solving and analysis at the community level. One of the first requirements is a coordinated effort among individuals, organizations, and agencies. Chapter 5 has dealt with the topic of coordination, but the need for cooperation and coordination cannot be overstressed.

Another requirement is to make better use of already existing skills and talents. Professional educators, planning specialists, and governmental officials are only some of the people in each community who have skills and experiences in decision-making and problem-solving. These people could take the lead in analyzing various problems and could lend invaluable assistance in planning corresponding programs directed toward providing solutions.

Another important requirement in analyzing community problems and needs is to determine just what is the nature of the particular problems. Here is a good opportunity to involve the local citizen in community and educational programs. Individual residents and various groups, such as the PTA, service organizations, and public agencies, can be involved through study groups, discussion clubs, community surveys, and advisory councils. Later sections describe the use of community surveys and advisory councils in greater detail.

Study groups or discussion clubs may be made up of only community residents who make recommendations to agencies and organizations administering community educational or change-related programs; or, residents and various professionals may cooperate on specific tasks. However, to determine the relationship between various problems and needs of the total community, people that represent all age, socioeconomic, and racial groups should be involved.

Relating problem solution to education and the schools, the following are examples of typical community problems that groups and individuals might study:

1. How to activate the educative community — What resources are available? Who should be involved? What would it cost?
2. How to initiate a community school program — What additional costs would be required? What programs are needed and what could be added?
3. How to relate occupational needs with training — What are youth and young adults currently being trained for? What are the training requirements for various jobs? Can people be encouraged to undertake the training necessary for various jobs?
4. How to meet the many needs of adults living in an environment of change — What family life and human relationship skills are needed? Can adult and continuing education meet various needs? What will it cost for the continual education of adults?

Another requirement in community problem-solving that usually follows the study of particular problems is developing programs to meet the various needs. The local citizen can be involved at this point, too, through advisory roles, by assisting with the implementation of programs, and by providing feedback information to program planners and agency administrators as to whether or not their needs are being met. The next section expands on the use of various community residents in carrying out educational or change programs.

A final requirement to be described concerns further developing the community problem-solving skills of community residents and leaders. This can be accomplished in two basic ways. One way is to provide various opportunities for parents and other residents to gain experience in problem analysis and program-planning. Schools can do this through parent groups, advisory councils, and parental involvement in curriculum development.

Another way to develop these skills is for communities to establish courses or formal experiences related to problem-solving. For example, some communities currently provide regular leader training sessions for volunteer youth workers. This type of leadership skill might be useful for a variety of community needs. Hopefully, the public schools or community colleges in many communities will begin to provide classroom instruction for adults that will deal with techniques for solving problems and for facilitating community change.

STRATEGIES FOR ACHIEVING CHANGE

To achieve changes in communities through education may require efforts by various people or organizations. Nor is any single approach likely to accomplish all of its goals or objectives. Consequently, it may be necessary to employ a variety of strategies in planning and implementing programs for educational or community change.

There are many different strategies, tactics, or approaches that can be utilized to achieve community change. Not all of them can be discussed in a book of this nature. Only four will be described in this section; you may wish to refer to some of the sources at the conclusion of the chapter for additional information.

One strategy for achieving change is to learn who are the community influentials or leaders, to understand how they affect the decision-making process, and to establish an acquaintanceship or friendship with them. Research and experience has shown that communities have individuals who control or greatly influence the decision-making that occurs. Individuals or groups who propose or plan programs of community change need to involve or consult these influential persons. An example might be a community school director studying the influentials that can affect the neighborhood in which he works in order to know whom to consult or involve in establishing new programs. Learning how to identify the community's influentials and understanding the dynamics of the decision-making process should increase the effectiveness of attempts to achieve changes.

Another strategy is to identify with and utilize existing groups and organizations that will support community change attempts. Sometimes referred to as intervention or planned change, this approach involves the coordination of two or more groups on a program of change. A professional planner or expert is frequently utilized to promote this cooperation. An illustration would be the community college and public school system of a community cooperating on a campaign to win public support for a new basketball fieldhouse to be shared by both. A public relations or planning expert might be hired or an educational employee temporarily released from some other educational duty to coordinate the campaign.

A third strategy sometimes employed to achieve a change is to affiliate with an organization whose function can include directing or guiding change programs. These organizations often perform a change-agent role, where their employees are skilled at the means utilized to achieve various changes or goals. Change agents have been referred to as catalysts, enablers, or stimulators, and they possess skills in human relations, the diagnosis of problems, and the adaptation of various resources to achieve a program's goals. For example, the public school administrator might ask the county cooperative extension agent to develop and coordinate a program to involve inner city youth in some after-school programs. The county agent would develop a program that utilized volunteer parents and other citizens as leaders and teachers.

A final strategy to be described is to form committees or groups around particular content areas or particular needs. This would involve the cooperation of an agency or organization that possessed various physical and organizational resources with groups that possessed special skills and/or an accessibility to a particular clientele. This might be especially useful in providing education to meet unique minority-group needs. For example, a community school director in a predominantly Mexican-American community could form a neighborhood group of Mexican-American parents. The community school could provide various resources and the parent group could direct a tutorial program to those youngsters and adults who require it.

The above approaches are some of those available for people and organizations interested in achieving some type of community change through education. Each might be successful or might fail, depending on the community and the people involved. A successful application of any strategy will be facilitated by a thorough knowledge of the community and by utilizing the input of the community's residents.

KNOWING AND USING THE COMMUNITY

No single educator can know and understand all that needs to be known about a community. Consequently, to gain a more complete understanding of the community, some means of acquiring information must be employed. This section will describe two of these means: The community council and the community survey. Additional methods of acquiring information and of understanding the dynamics of particular communities are suggested in various references at the conclusion of the chapter.

Community Councils

There are three primary reasons why a community council might be formed. One is that the community has a particular problem to be solved and the involvement of various community residents is sought in solving it. Another reason is that a problem is too large for any one organization to handle alone and the utilization of various resources is required for finding solutions. A third reason is the desire of educators to obtain advice and information from various community representatives in order to plan and implement programs that will meet a majority of needs.

This last reason can be illustrated by what takes place in most community schools. Community school directors typically set up neighborhood advisory committees or councils as a way of obtaining regular information and assistance on educational programs and needs. An advisory committee will not automatically guarantee a successful community school program but without it the lines of communication between a school and the community are limited.

What is the makeup of a community council? A typical council might have 12 to 20 community representatives. Figure 1 shows various organizations and groups that could be represented on a community or advisory council. Above all, citizens from all age groups, from all types of organizations, and from all walks of life should be included to provide a fair sample of community interests and opinions.

The functions of a community council can be many. They can range from strictly advisory to decision-making. An important role for every council is to provide a line of communication between local citizens and their needs and the people administering community and educational programs. For example, as was illustrated in Chapter 3, a community school director utilizes advisory committee input as one important source of the information required to plan programs.

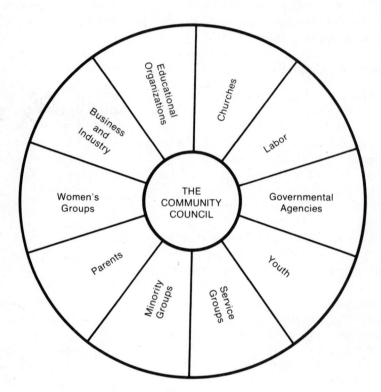

Figure 1. Community Council Representation

Another function can be actual problem-solving: Councils will often divide into smaller ad hoc groups or individual council members will provide the leadership in forming small study and action groups for purposes of examining a particular problem. Recommendations for solutions can be made directly to educational organizations or some councils will have the authority and resources to implement programs.

Councils often function as advisory bodies in the development of educational policy. For example, one community council studied the educational needs of older and retired citizens for several months. They eventually recommended the following that required changes in policy: (1) the community college should offer several courses to senior citizens in retirement homes or in senior citizen centers; (2) the public school adult education department should eliminate all course and program fees for every person retired and/or over sixty-five; and (3) the local businesses and industries should institute a continuous and regular pre-retirement training program for employees fifty years of age or older.

A final function of councils to be described here is that of assisting in the evaluation of educational programs. Evaluation can be in terms of assessing whether a program or course is achieving its objectives or whether a program is actually meeting some community need. A council could even isolate a particular problem, such as those of high school dropouts or unemployment, and assess whether educational programs exist to solve them and, if so, whether they are successful.

There are various ways of increasing a council's level of contribution to its community. For example, council members can be trained in various skill areas that will relate to their functions such as community assessment, evaluation, and communications. Another example is to provide council members feedback on the services they are performing to promote a feeling of confidence that their efforts will be useful. In whatever ways councils are used, trained, or supported, they provide a potential means to bring education and the community closer together.

Community Surveys

The solution of community problems by the efforts of one individual or even by one agency is largely a thing of the past. Most problems affect all people of a community and therefore require the involvement of many for their solution. Pollution bothers the young and the old. Unemployment is critical for females as well as for males. A lack of education affects those in the inner city as well as those living in suburbs.

Assessing the various needs of a community and of its residents is an important prelude to solving problems. For example, if educators are going to coordinate the planning and implementing of various community education programs, they must have some means of acquiring information on needs and preferences.

The community survey has become a popular means of acquiring information for decision-making and program-planning. The survey is used to gather information that will indicate the attitudes of people regarding their educational concerns. It can also be used to assess a community's physical and human resources. A survey might even be utilized to determine the nature of horizontal or vertical relationships as a basis for assessing future support for educational programs.

There are several dimensions of a community that can be studied. The following dimensions are suggested as those most useful in understanding a community and its needs:[1]

1. Population factors—the percentage of people in various age and other groupings, the educational backgrounds of people, and the extent of mobility in and out of the community—to provide an analysis of the existing human resources.
2. Institutional structure—the various existing groups, organizations, and agencies, their membership makeup, and their organizational purposes—to analyze the extent and complexity of social relationships and to examine the range of available educational opportunity.
3. Value system—the hospitality, relationship between people, security, traditions, and beliefs—to determine the values and attitudes possessed toward education or other areas.
4. Social class structure—the identifiable structure of people according to income, race, religion, or educational background—to assess potential participation by various population groups in certain educational and community programs and to analyze the informal or social relationships between people.
5. Economic structure—the range of incomes, the problems of inadequate incomes, the concentration of economic leadership, and the general use of the community—to analyze the decision-making process, the potential support for educational and community programs, and the functioning of people within the community.

[1]Adapted from Gordon W. Blackwell, "The Needs of the Community as a Determinant of Evening College," *1953 Proceedings* (St. Louis: Association of University Evening Colleges, 1953). A revised version also appears in *Purposes of the Evening College* (Boston: Center for the Study of Liberal Education for Adults, 1967).

A community survey will involve first the determining of agencies or groups to conduct the survey. This might include a community council, various interested agencies, or a professional group with surveying skills. Another important step is to identify the various groups, institutions, and people to be examined, depending on the purpose and extent of the survey. The determination or development of various information-collecting instruments also is an important part of the survey process. Several of the sources at the conclusion of the chapter provide a discussion or example of various questionnaires, check lists, or survey items.

The collection of information through a community survey is only the beginning of the process. The information will need to be processed, analyzed, and interpreted. The interpreted information will then become the basis for planning and implementing various programs. It is anticipated that the community survey can provide information vital for sound decision-making and the solution of community problems.

MODELS OF COMMUNITY CHANGE

Obtaining a knowledge and understanding of the community is only the beginning of planning and implementing programs of change directed at specific problems. Various phases of the planning process must be recognized and carried out. The purpose of this section is to describe various community change models, to identify the phases common to most models, and to suggest a planning model that would be applicable to most communities.

Table 1 displays the phases of several community change models. Although each author's description of what takes place during each phase is somewhat unique, there are actually many similarities between the models. The reader is referred to the bibliographic citation for each author at the conclusion of this chapter to obtain a detailed discussion of the various models.

What are the similarities and commonalities between various models of community change? A first phase usually involves an analysis of the situation leading up to or causing the problem. This phase is exploratory, where the needs of people are assessed, the commonality of interest is analyzed, and the initial problem is defined or described. The information obtained in a community survey could be quite helpful during this phase.

The second phase is typically the initial efforts at organizing and planning for problem solution. The establishment of program goals,

Table 1. Some Models of Community Change (adapted from original sources by authors — see bibliography)

Author	I	II	III	IV	V	VI
SOWER	Convergence of Interest	Initiating of Action	Legitimation and Sponsorship	Development of Plan	Organization	Implement and Evaluate
BIDDLE	Exploratory Process	Organizational	Discussional	± ———— Action ———— ±		New Projects or Continue
WARREN	Initial Environment	± ——— Inception of the Action ——— ±		Expansion of the Action	Operation of the Action	Transformation of the Action
BEAL	The Social System / Convergence of Interest	Prior Social System / Relevant Social System / Initiating Sets	Legitimation Act / Diffusion	Definition of Need / Decision to Act	Goals and Objectives / Means / Plan of Work / Organizing Resources	Implementation Act / Evaluation
SANDERS	Idea Takes Root / Obtain the Facts	± ———— Plan Program of Action Based on Facts ———— ±		± —— Launch and Move Program Forward —— ± / ± —— Continually Take Your Bearings —— ±		Summarize
LIPPITT	Client Discovers Need for Help	Helping Relationship Is Defined	Change Problem Is Identified and Clarified	Change Efforts Are Attempted	Change Becomes Generalized and Stabilized	Helping Relationship Ends or Continuing Relationship Is Defined

objectives, and priorities is usually accomplished during this phase. The development of educational programs will often involve the utilization of objectives written in terms of change in human behavior.

A third phase involves the assessment of community support toward attempts to solve particular problems. This might include obtaining some form of legitimation from the community's influential citizens or leaders and/or from the community council. It could also involve obtaining financial and organizational sponsorship.

The next phase includes organizing and planning the program of change. The community survey information or a community council's input could provide some assessment of the resources available to the program. The overall plan, time schedule, and description of the required physical and human resources are usually included; they normally are based on the goals, objectives, and priorities established earlier.

The fifth phase common to many models is the actual implementation of the change program. If the prior phases have been completed carefully, the success of this phase will be greatly facilitated. It is important to note that a great deal of time and effort needs to be invested before the implementation of a program can successfully take place.

A final phase, and an important one, is that of evaluation. Evaluation is essential in determining to what extent the change program actually met the need or solved the problem for which it was designed. Many models will include in this phase some method of feeding back the evaluation information to those who assisted with the program, to the sponsors, and to the general community population. This phase could also involve some decision-making as to whether the change program should be continued or redone.

It is suggested that the six phases described above can be utilized by many communities in designing their own community or educational programs of change. The following model summarizes the various phases:

1. Analysis of the problem situation.
2. Goal and objective setting.
3. Assessment of the commitment to proceed.
4. Organizing and planning the program.
5. Implementing the program.
6. Evaluating the program.

These phases will not exactly fit the planning needs of each community. The information is presented primarily as a guide to planning attempts. Adaptations and additions may be required. The phases do not always have to follow the sequence suggested, depending on the unique requirements of a community. However, the failure of most community programs and activities can be traced to one or more of the phases not receiving enough consideration.

This chapter has only briefly introduced the multitude of information related to the process of community change. The successful planning of programs for community change requires a wealth of community information, the utilization of various strategies and techniques, and a systematic design of the processes to be attempted. Furthermore, it is suggested that developing a close relationship between the educational system and the community for purposes of solving community and societal problems makes imperative the understanding and utilization of change theory and methodology.

SOME DEFINITIONS

Change Agent—Persons or agency representatives who instigate purposeful social action.

Community Influentials (also known as key leaders, power actors, or legitimizers) — Individuals who play a major role in community decision-making. These people can and do influence changes made in a community.

Community Change (also known as social action, social change, or community action)—A relatively formal, deliberate, organized, and short-term attempt to promote some type of change in a community and/or its residents.

Intervention or Planned Change—The development of specific strategies for achieving specific change objectives. This often involves a person with professional planning skills being supported by some community agency in promoting a change attempt.

SELECTED BIBLIOGRAPHY

ALINSKY, SAUL D. *Reveille for Radicals*. Chicago: University of Chicago Press, 1946. 228 pages. Considered one of the early advocates of the poor, the author presents his philosophy, principles, and tactics for social change. He discusses what he means by radicalism and the role that it needs to play in the alleviation of social, economic, and political plight. He also describes the building of a people's organization. Included in the book are discussions on indigenous community leadership, how to understand the community, and how to use community knowledge in promoting social change.

AMERICAN LIBRARY ASSOCIATION. *Studying the Community*. Washington, D.C.: American Library Association, 1960. 128 pages. Appendixes. This book describes how to carry out a community survey. It discusses the roles of various people, the sources of information, the techniques for collecting information, and the processes for interpreting the information. The appendixes contain a variety of example questionnaires and survey helps.

BAUMEL, C. PHILLIP; HOBBS, DARYL J.; and POWERS, RONALD C. *The Community Survey*. Ames, Iowa: Iowa State University, Cooperative Extension Service, Soc. 15, 1964. 65 pages. Appendix. This publication describes the methods of community surveying as a means of gathering information useful in decision-making. It discusses how to organize for a community survey, how to develop information-collecting devices, and how to collect, tabulate, and interpret the information. Especially useful are several sample community survey questions.

BEAL, GEORGE M., *et al. Social Action and Interaction in Program Planning*. Ames, Iowa: Iowa State University Press, 1966. 510 pages. Index. Bibliography. The objective of this book was to analyze the process of introducing and applying an experimental approach in educationally related program planning. Several principles of program planning are included. The authors also present and describe an extensive model of social action.

BENNIS, WARREN G.; BENNE, KENNETH D.; and CHIN, ROBERT (eds.). *The Planning of Change*. New York: Holt, Rinehart and Winston, Inc., 1969. 421 pages. Index. This is a book of readings reflecting the theory, research, and practical application of behavioral science knowledge as it applies to change. Discussions and evaluations of the body of change technologies are included. A discussion of the change agent, planned change elements, dynamics of planned change, and values and goals as they relate to change are some of the topics covered.

HAND, SAMUEL E. *An Outline of a Community Survey for Program Planning in Adult Education*. Bulletin No. 71f-2, revised. Tallahasee, Florida: Florida State Department of Education, 1968. 45 pages. This bulletin delineates the kinds of information about a community that would be helpful in planning adult education programs, such as the history of the community, the economic structure, and the sources of information. Also discussed is the issue of participation in organized community programs as a way of solving problems.

HOIBERG, OTTO G. *Exploring the Small Community*. Lincoln, Nebraska: University of Nebraska Press, 1955. 199 pages. Index. This book was written primarily to assist those interested in studying small, rural communities. It covers a wide range of topics, including understanding and studying the small community, planning community activities, and developing community leaders. The second part of the book, which deals with understanding various agencies, organizations, or problem topics in the small community, will be especially useful.

LIPPITT, RONALD; WATSON, JEANNE; and WESTLEY, BRUCE. *The Dynamics of Planned Change*. New York: Harcourt, Brace and Company, 1958. Index. Bibliography. The authors present a series of chapters designed to prepare a change agent for the task of instituting planned change programs. They center their discussion on such topics as diagnosing community relationships, motivating people toward change, understanding various phases of planned change, and training professional change agents.

MCMAHON, ERNEST E. *Needs — of People and Their Communities — and the Adult Educator*. Washington, D.C.: Adult Education Association of the USA, 1970. 50 pages. Bibliography. This booklet is designed as a text for community workers. It suggests how the needs of people can be assessed and how to utilize the acquired information in program planning. An important part of the booklet is an extensive annotated bibliography of many articles and books related to need assessment and program planning.

POWERS, RONALD C. *Identifying the Community Power Structure*. North Central Regional Extension Publication No. 19, NCRS-5 Leadership Series No. 2. Ames, Iowa: Iowa State University, Cooperative Extension Service, Soc. 18, 1965. 11 pages. Selected Bibliography. This bulletin draws upon the research and experience of sociologists in presenting a technique for the identification of key influentials or power figures in a community. It also provides some discussion of the role community power figures play in decision-making.

SOWER, CHRISTOPHER, *et al. Community Involvement*. Glencoe, Illinois: The Free Press, 1957. 323 pages. Bibliography. This book describes the strategy for directed social action. A sequence of events and the social processes utilized in social action are explained. The material will help the reader better understand how to plan and instigate community change.

WARREN, ROLAND L. *Studying Your Community*. New York: Russell Sage Foundation, 1955. 385 pages. Index. This book is presented as a manual for people interested in studying their own community. The chapters provide a factual basis for the community and suggest organizational, planning, and action programs that can be applied to the community. A discussion of the American community, its various institutions, and carrying out community surveys are some of the topics covered.

From other chapters:

CHAPTER 7

Community Investments in Education

The discussion in the preceding chapters has concentrated on describing the community, its educative potential, and how the school and family can benefit from the realization of this potential. Education has primarily been referred to in general terms, as a process involving people of all ages. The purpose of this chapter is to describe education in more specific terms so that community leaders and decision-makers will have a basis for planning where the scarce educational dollar can be utilized.

EXAMINING INVESTMENTS IN EDUCATION

During the past decade or longer a great deal has been said about the need for community growth and expansion. American communities have been made aware of this need by experts of all description, by governmental officials, by politicians, and by officials of various industrial and commercial corporations. Consequently, one aspect of American society upon which widespread agreement can now be found is that communities continuously attempt various measures to promote growth.

An important contributor to growth and development is a community's own human resources. Skilled workers must be available if various adults are to keep up with societal or technological changes that affect their jobs. Management and leadership training programs must be developed if community and business leaders are to maintain and improve their abilities to solve various problems. Thus, if the goals of communities and society are to be realized, human resource development is a necessary condition for achieving them.

The level of human resource development, therefore, can be used as an indicator of a community's readiness for growth. The identification of various educational investments directed toward developing human resources will not explain all the elements required to promote growth and development. Some of the variables difficult to control or measure are understanding the community, activating the educative community, utilizing the school as a community center, helping families to better utilize education, and promoting a close coordination between all portions of community life. However, it is expected that the ability to appraise investments in education will assist communities in planning and promoting a more satisfying life for their citizens.

The value of education to an individual usually centers on his or her ability to earn a living and the opportunity or preparation to obtain still further education. The high school graduate will have more opportunities for a better job than the school dropout, and the high school diploma is now a standard prerequisite for acceptance into higher forms of education. Once on the job, the more highly educated employees are typically the first chosen for advanced training and the first to be promoted to better jobs at higher salaries.

The advantages of a sound education on the job can extend beyond higher incomes and promotion opportunities. Greater receptivity to new ideas and changes on the job is usually found in higher educated employees. This is critical to the adaptation required to keep current with rapid change and necessary for community growth. In addition, the educational level of one worker may also have favorable effects on the productivity of fellow workers. Whenever production involves cooperation among employees, the flexibility and adaptability of one worker will usually be an advantage to others.

The benefits of education can also extend to the family of an individual. The informal education received in the home and the attitudes obtained toward learning, for example, are related to the educational level of the parents.

At the community level, residents can be affected favorably by the values developed in children through education and the home. The larger society is benefited by the development of an informed and responsible citizenry. These benefits can in turn be realized by the general taxpayer where education has reduced the need to support the results of a lack of education, such as unemployment, crime, delinquency, and poverty.

Thus, investments in education, if of the right kinds and in the right amounts, can have economic benefits and yield even a social return on the dollar. The challenge becomes one of improving the educational system we now have. To this end, educational and community decision-makers must continue to improve their knowledge and understanding of the role human resource development plays in the dynamics of community growth and change.

Whether all citizens can be helped to have a more satisfying life merely by making correct investments in education is a point for speculation. Perhaps it is idealistic to think that many community or societal problems can be totally corrected by better trained and more skilled human resources. However, the need for educators, community leaders, and other citizens to understand how education is and can be related to the quality of total community life hopefully has been made clear in earlier chapters.

For example, at the local community level many decisions are made regularly that affect education and the level of human resource development. Yet, such decisions are often based on tradition or assumed needs. In addition, decisions made at the state or national level often affect or supersede local decisions, causing confusion and overlap of programs.

The recent occurrence of several programs outside the educational system that are designed to prepare human resources is further indication that decisions affecting communities are not coordinated. Community action programs, special training programs, and private training programs are just some of the many examples of this "shotgun" approach to education. The central coordinating agency described in Chapter 5 might provide the leadership necessary to correct this overlapping of educational investment.

The result of overlap, duplication, and confusion often has been either an over-investment or an under-investment in education. A recent aspect of an over-investment has been the apparent surplus of certain kinds of teachers. Some teachers, for example, have not been able to secure a teaching position, or, they have had to accept an opening some distance from where they wanted to settle.

Under-investment is being forced on several school systems throughout America. The current economic situation and/or other reasons have resulted in bond failures, millage defeats, and a general decreasing support for education in some communities. In extreme cases, schools have been forced to eliminate extracurricular activities, to initiate half-day programs, and to greatly increase teacher-pupil ratios.

What is now needed is a systematic approach to educational investment that can be utilized along with efforts to activate the entire community. Therefore, the purpose of this chapter is to provide a framework for educational investments that will promote and facilitate decision-making. This framework will describe four categories of education in which investments can be made. The information should help community leaders and interested citizens concerned with education to gain some increased understanding of the requirements necessary to develop adequate human resources.

A PROPER COMBINATION OF INVESTMENTS IN EDUCATION

Determining the nature and amount of educational investments required for promoting community growth and for improving the lives of all residents has many complexities. First, there is a notion shared by some community leaders that growth will result simply from a continual increase in educational investments: "We need a new high school building!" "A new community college fieldhouse will be good for the town!" "What we need is an enlarged public library system!" Actually, there is no predictable or clear-cut relationship between the amount of investments in education and any resulting growth. In reality, educational investments of the wrong kind may impede growth.

Second, the idea exists that investments in education should be made only after investments in economic development have been completed. "The new community auditorium should have priority over a new school building!" "Encouraging new industry to move to a community should be done before a community school program is developed!" However, the provision of trained people for any new jobs that are created may require a tremendous investment in education, and the success of new economic ventures may depend on the educational potential of a community. Therefore, it becomes just as logical to begin with a strategy for the development of human resources and then work to maximize community growth based on the effectiveness of the educational system.

Consequently, what must be involved in any community planning efforts is a close relationship between the educational system and the economy. The process of planning for educational investments must include determining the potential value, in economic terms, of different amounts and types of education. Assuming that the goal of educational investments is human resource development, there are four general types of educational enterprises in which investments should be made: (1) Formal education, (2) occupational education, (3) continuing and adult education, and (4) community development. The proper combination of investments in each is essential to a community's growth and development.

Formal Education

Formal education begins with the primary school and concludes with the higher forms of education and training. This includes those institutions or agencies specializing in the production of training, as distinct from those organizations offering training or education in conjunction with learning a skill necessary for the production of goods or the performance of an occupational service. Some institutions, such as those training technicians, specialize in mainly one skill area, while others, such as universities, offer a large and diverse selection of skill areas.

Investments in formal education are made in elementary and secondary schools, colleges, universities, and professional schools, where the education is part of a continuous and long-range program to supply knowledge as a basis for participation in society outside of the school setting. Vocational education that encompasses instruction at the secondary school level and is designed to provide exploration opportunities in various careers, pre-employment training in nonprofessional and low-skill jobs, cooperative work-study opportunities, and skills in the practical arts is considered part of formal education. For the most part, participants in these various forms of education are removed from productive economic roles.

Occupational Education

Investment in occupational education is a large component of many communities' total educational investment. Participants in these kinds of programs receive specialized occupational training related to the performance of their present or future work roles. Simulated work settings in laboratories and shops (machine shops, electronic laboratories, dental laboratories, etc.) are provided for students at the upper high school, community college, technical college, and graduate or professional university levels. Actual on-the-job instruction is provided in such settings as industries, offices, stores, and hospitals.

Growth occurs as individuals increase their productivity potential by acquiring new skills or perfecting old ones while on the job or in a simulated job setting. The range of complexity in acquiring skills is quite extensive. For example, the apprentice learns a new skill while combining on-the-job training and trade related instruction. The medical intern, on the other hand, develops those skills he acquired in medical school. Both type of workers are more productive as a result of this form of educational investment. Therefore, occupational education is a process of raising future productivity and differs from the formal education investment in that learning takes place in a job setting rather than in a strictly classroom setting at the K-12 or college level.

Continuing and Adult Education

The third type of educational enterprise is continuing and adult education. This includes those processes whereby the adults in a community acquire the knowledge, understanding, attitudes, and skills necessary for adequate participation in a constantly changing society. Continuing and adult education, therefore, encompasses a wide variety of programs and activities. Participants in these programs typically hold jobs and/or occupy productive family roles within a community setting. Their participation is coordinated with daily activities in such a way that occupational and family commitments are continued.

The easily recognizable continuing education programs in most communities include adult high school, public school adult education, various community agencies' continuing education programs, and private adult education courses and programs. In addition, various kinds of retraining programs can be found in many communities. Some will be designed for the unemployed who must learn new skills; some will be for the highly skilled who must keep in touch with new developments in their fields; and some will be for those adults who simply wish to increase their skills and knowledge or who wish to change their career specialities.

Investments in continuing and adult education are important beyond intellectual stimulation or job upgrading. The continuing education enterprise must also play a corrective role for investment deficiencies in other types of education. This is especially important for the basic education, training, and job counseling of under-educated or under-employed adults. Consequently, most communities have a need to invest in adult basic education (ABE) programs.

Community Development

The fourth kind of educational investment shall be termed community development. Spontaneous changes, primarily induced by technological advances, will continuously occur in the American community. In response to these changes, internal adjustments must be made if a community is to maintain conditions which are supportive of growth and development. Therefore, community development investments are used to promote in people behavioral and organizational skills necessary for coping with change and for contributing to community growth.

The realm of community development includes many of the skills and techniques described in the preceding chapter. Developing community problem-solving and community change skills, training community leaders, studying the community, and promoting community action programs could all be classified as community development functions. Additional components would include mass media informational programs, informational literature, agency outreach programs, and study groups devoted to examining community problems or to developing the skills and procedures for removing such problems as roadblocks to community growth.

Suggested Levels of Community Investments in Education[1]

Recognition of the important contribution education can make to economic and community growth has encouraged scholars to develop a rational basis for investing in education. The following suggestions present one viewpoint to consider in seeking a logical basis from which to make decisions and judgments pertaining to spending that educational dollar. Additional information on educational investment models and various viewpoints on investing in education are presented in several of the sources contained in the bibliography at the conclusion of this chapter.

The suggestions to be described cannot show exactly what should be done in every community or in what proportion investments should be made in each different educational enterprise. However, it is hoped that the suggested investment levels will enable community residents and decision-makers to better understand the need to consider where and in what proportion investments in education should be made.

The suggestions are based on the four areas of educational investment described in the preceding section. Furthermore, the urban community of 50,000 people or more is the basis for the suggested investments. Smaller or rural communities may need to consider alternative models or different proportions. Finally, the framework of

[1]These suggestions were adapted from the work by Gale E. Jensen in Gale E. Jensen and William K. Medlin (eds.), *Readings on the Planning of Education for Community and National Development,* Problems in Education and Nation Building, Vol. I (Ann Arbor, Michigan: Ann Arbor Publishers, 1969).

suggestions presented is still at a theoretical level of development. Only a few communities have been studied with these investment levels as a research basis. Additional study and utilization will be required to refine the material and to relate the investment levels even closer to the four educational investment enterprises. Until this refinement process is complete, the material can be used only as a geneṛal guide to the decisions made at a community level.

The aim of educational investment in a community seeking to promote growth and development should be that of developing and maintaining an adequate human resource supply both in terms of quality and quantity. Thus, up to 15 percent of a community's available money and resources should be invested in education. For example, a community with an annual gross national product equivalent to $10,000,000 would invest approximately $1.5 million in education.[2] These monies, then, would be invested in the four educational enterprises in the following manner. (Table 1 displays the recommended investment proportions for the above described dollar amount.)

Table 1. Recommended Investment Percentages in the Four Investment Areas (1.5 million dollars is used as an example for the calculations)

INVESTMENT AREA	RECOMMENDED PERCENTAGE	DOLLAR AMOUNT
Formal Education	40-50%	$600,000-750,000*
Continuing and Adult Education	30-40%	$450,000-600,000*
Occupational Education	15%	$225,000
Community Development	5%	$ 75,000
Total Investment		$1,500,000

*It is assumed that any trade-off in investment will come between formal education and continuing and adult education.

It is suggested, for example, that 40-50 percent of the total community investment in education should be made in formal education. This investment will range from providing the basic literacy training of the young to preparing young adults through high school or college for their roles in the community. It will also provide the general occupational preparation of a large percentage of the population.

[2]Determining the money available in a community will require some knowledge and understanding of its economy and of economic analysis. Some suggested economic measures that can be determined or found for most communities are a community Gross National Product, Effective Buying Income (see the *Sales Management* magazine), or the per capita income of residents.

Another 30-40 percent of the educational dollar should be invested in continuing and adult education. These monies will be necessary for the in-service training of high-level professionals or for retraining programs designed to correct imbalances that occur in the supply of human resources. A portion of this investment will also be used for the basic, vocational, and family-life training of the under-educated and under-employed community members in an attempt to improve the quality of their personal and family living.

Occupational education also has a great deal of potential in promoting and continuing community growth. It is suggested that approximately 15 percent of the monies earmarked for education should be allocated to this educational area. The purpose will be to make available a constantly upgraded work force capable of undertaking or adapting to occupations as they become available or change.

The investment in community development should be approximately 5 percent of the total community budget for education. These monies will need to be utilized to analyze community problems and to help community members become aware of how these problems affect a community's growth potential. This money will also be utilized to provide various residents with leadership and problem-solving skills.

IMPLICATIONS FOR COMMUNITY INVESTMENT IN EDUCATION

The material presented in this chapter has only been an introduction to the rationale for making various investments in education. Measuring the current level of investments being made by communities has not been discussed. In addition, the planning process that must take place prior to making any community investments was not presented. Various sources in the bibliography at the conclusion of the chapter provide some guidance on these needs.

The commitment to invest in education does not depend only on the desire a community might have for education or on some logical framework for making investments in various educational enterprises. Numerous factors, such as the density and makeup of the population, the standard of community living, and the occupational background of the residents affect the decisions that must be made. In addition, any investments made in education will not have an immediate impact on the community. Rather, change or response to any different emphasis will be gradual over a long period of time.

Whether all or even some of the many problems facing communities can be corrected by intelligent investments in education is unknown at this point, However, the need for community leaders, educators, and interested citizens to understand more about the investment process hopefully has been made apparent. A greater utilization of the community for educational purposes will depend, in part, on a careful coordination and planning of the amount and kind of investment in education.

SELECTED BIBLIOGRAPHY

BENSON, CHARLES S. *Perspectives on the Economics of Education.* Boston: Houghton Mifflin Company, 1963. 477 pages. This is a book of readings that cover a wide range of topics related to investing in education. The book is directed toward the school administrator, but interested parents and community leaders will also find it informative. The general topics covered include the following: returns to education, economic structure of education, taxation, grants-in-aid, and problems of productivity in education.

BERGEVIN, PAUL. *A Philosophy for Adult Education.* New York: The Seabury Press, 1967. 176 pages. Index. Selected reading list. The author addresses himself to several problem areas in adult education. Such problems as the resistance to change, the under-educated citizen, and the difficulty of motivating adults to participate in adult and continuing education activities are discussed. The reader will gain some feeling for the investment needs in adult and continuing education.

DAVIS, RUSSELL G. *Planning Human Resource Development.* Chicago: Rand McNally & Company, 1966. 334 pages. Index. Bibliography. Appendixes. This book introduces and discusses various models, schemata, and methods for human resource development. The book is written primarily for economists and community leaders. It contains several mathematical formulas and explanations as supplemental material.

FANTINI, MARIO D., and YOUNG, MILTON A. *Designing Education for Tomorrow's Cities.* New York: Holt, Rinehart and Winston, Inc., 1970. 160 pages. Index. Bibliography. Appendixes. This book advocates a system of education that stresses the human aspect of education. The authors define education in system terms and present the system as if it were to be applied to a newly developed community. The reader will gain some understanding of the investment requirements for the educational dollar.

HARBISON, FREDERICK, and MYERS, CHARLES A. *Education, Manpower, and Economic Growth.* New York: McGraw-Hill Book Company, 1964. 229 pages. Index. The authors develop some concepts related to human resource development. Some of the topics dealt with are problems and issues, strategies for human resource development, planning for development, and integrating human resource and general development. An important contribution is one chapter which deals with the development of some quantitative indicators for measuring human resource development.

JENSEN, GALE E., and MEDLIN, WILLIAM K. (eds.). *Readings on the Planning of Education for Community and National Development.* Problems in Education and Nation Building, Vol. I. Ann Arbor, Michigan: Ann Arbor Publishers, 1969. 81 pages. This book, the first in a series designed around the relationship between education and community growth, presents some readings on planning for education. Both foreign and domestic examples are utilized. A chapter by Jensen describes his four-phase conceptual model for the investment of educational dollars in human resource development.

ROBERTS, ROY W. *Vocational and Practical Arts Education.* New York: Harper & Row, Publishers, 1971. 500 pages. Index. Appendixes. This book provides a comprehensive examination of the current developments in vocational education. Emphasis is placed on the origins, development, principles, and relationships of these areas of education. The reader will gain some understanding of the needed investments in formal and occupational education.

WEISBROD, BURTON A. *External Benefits of Public Education.* Princeton, New Jersey: Princeton University, Industrial Relations Section, Department of Economics, 1964. 144 pages. Appendixes. This book explores the extent to which education provides benefits to people. A conceptual analysis of the benefits in a decentralized educational system is included. Tables and appendixes are utilized to illustrate the concepts being presented.

CHAPTER 8

Higher Education and the Community

This last chapter is not intended to be a summary of the preceding chapters, although it relates closely to them. Rather, a discussion of higher education is a natural topic with which to conclude this book. Institutions of higher education must be involved in, and committed to, solving the various problems of communities and society if efforts at the local level are to be successful. The activation of the educative community cannot take place unless professional educators are involved; these educators can receive their motivation and training for community involvement from our colleges and universities.

Consequently, the purpose of this chapter is to discuss the role of higher education in today's society. This role is partially based on traditional heritage; in other ways, it is based on a constant evolvement in conjunction with rapid societal change. Most of the chapter will argue that a greater community emphasis is needed and will present some ideas and suggestions for implementing this emphasis.

ROLE OF THE UNIVERSITY

The American university or college is primarily a reflection of the society in which it exists. This has resulted in most institutions of higher education patterning their programs after a society based on rapid population growth, technological advance, and constant social change. Consequently, universities and colleges have usually experienced constant growth and expansion over the past two decades— growth that has not necessarily been carefully planned or based on urgent social needs.

Before a university can transform society, it must be transformed from within. Administrators, alumni, state legislators, and private supporters must realize and accept that the function of higher education should be the solution of societal problems, regardless of the cost, traditional direction, or required changes.

We need to help the university stand unique as an institution devoted to solving societal problems. If we believe that the community can become educationally activated, that education can solve community problems, and that a skilled human resource supply will be a leading force in keeping our society strong, then we must also believe in the university as a catalytic force for all of this.

Some specific ways higher education institutions currently attempt to meet societal needs are the following:

1. Educating people both at the undergraduate and graduate levels for citizenship roles.
2. Equipping people for successful careers.
3. Conducting research on a variety of problems.
4. Promoting the cultivation of the arts.
5. Preserving the freedom of intellectual pursuit.
6. Providing specialized service on needs outside the university.
7. Taking the lead in solving problems vital to survival.

Hopefully, each of the above processes will be continued without financial or societal constraints.

A final aspect of the university role in society to be described is a continuous evaluation of how universities and colleges are doing. This includes assessing what the universities and their graduates are doing in society and the community and utilizing this assessment information to make needed changes in the direction of higher education.

RESOURCES OF THE UNIVERSITY

Resources of universities and colleges are many. All have a potential for helping local communities solve their problems and meeting the needs of community residents. One important resource is the access to skilled and talented human resources. The educational skills and experiences of university employees can be utilized not only for internal instruction or administration but also for teaching, research, and service in local communities.

Another resource is the knowledge supply available to those who desire it. Library materials, research reports, and computer-stored information are basic assets of the modern university or college. This information can be applied to problem solution in a variety of ways.

Related to the above resource is the outreach potential of most higher education institutions. Many universities have existing outreach programs through cooperative extension and/or university extension services. These programs provide educational opportunities and assistance to certain clientele, and usually the only requirement for increasing the availability of this resource is financial support.

The primary resources of universities and colleges have been described to show the potential of service to communities. It is suggested that universities can and should play an even bigger role in society. Most of this enlarged role is needed in the form of assistance to local communities in helping them to understand and solve their problems. Consequently, the modern university and college must place a greater emphasis on community involvement. This includes service in helping community residents with various needs and in promoting in university graduates a greater commitment to education and assistance at the community level.

TRIPARTITE FUNCTIONS AND THE COMMUNITY

The role of the university is based on three traditional functions: teaching, research, and service. This section will discuss each of them. They will not be discussed in terms of what is currently taking place, as that varies significantly from university to university. Rather, the function will be discussed as it could be performed with the community and community education as basic frames of reference.

Starting with the Community

This subsection is included prior to describing the three functions to emphasize the importance of considering the community as a basis for planning university programs, rather than the other way around. One scholar has even suggested that universities be renamed as communiversities, where community needs and problems are the central focus points for university activities.

Just as we emphasized earlier the need to develop a sense of community in community residents and educators, there is a need for university personnel to understand what is a community and how it can be studied. The promotion of a positive attitude toward the community should facilitate the development of a feeling of community responsibility. This could then be reflected through research, service, and the attitudes developed by students in the college classroom.

Just as we suggested for educators at the community level, university employees should also learn what they can about youth and adults in their home and community settings. An understanding of community and family needs could result from this attempt to observe people where they live. For example, a chemist might conduct some research related to an observed nutritional problem. Or, a sociologist might bring his or her beginning students to a small, rural community so they could study social relationships and patterns. Finally, the schools of the inner city might be utilized as a learning laboratory for future teachers to learn how to create a community-centered classroom.

The Teaching Function

The teaching function of universities and colleges falls into two categories: the preparation of people for various careers and the training of people to be teachers. We will dwell primarily on this latter function, as a greater utilization of the community in education depends on the skills and attitudes of teachers working there.

The preparation of people for a multitude of occupations, however, is an important function of higher education. Here, too, a community orientation to learning can benefit communities and their problem-solving efforts. Thus, graduates of universities and colleges must know how to cope with change, must understand how to promote positive human relationships, and must have an understanding of their impact on a community and its problems. If university graduates are not committed to serving the communities in which they live and work, efforts to create a more satisfying life for all residents will be difficult to achieve.

Consequently, it is suggested that all students in higher education institutions need to be exposed to community theory and community education. This could be achieved through course work outside of their particular area of emphasis, through some type of off-campus exposure to the community, or through participation in a university-wide program of community action or service.

The preparation of teachers and school administrators requires a much larger exposure to the community if these educators are to perform successfully in contributing to the solution of community problems. A teacher must learn how to use the community as an educational resource, how to help parents and children use the community, and how to develop curricula that will help students understand the relationships between a particular subject and their life in the community.

As was described in earlier chapters, the teacher might serve in various roles in addition to classroom instruction: Change specialists, home visitation, and helping to solve certain community problems were some of those mentioned. Education at the college level should include information and experiences that will prepare teachers for these tasks.

Another teacher-training consideration should be the preparation of personnel who will be involved in community schools. Potential community school directors, counselors, administrators, and teachers all require exposure to the philosophy and concepts of the community school movement. Emphasizing a greater utilization of the community will include much of the information needed, but some universities may need to develop special courses and experiences to supplement a prospective teacher's program.

Teachers who will be involved in community schools or who wish to contribute to a greater utilization of education in the community will need exposure to a variety of teaching and learning approaches. Utilizing the community as a classroom requires a flexible approach to education; therefore, teachers must be skilled at promoting self-inquiry, at involving parents and students in curriculum development, and at the individualized instructional approach.

The training of teachers who plan to work in the inner city of large communities requires a somewhat different approach. Teachers hopefully will know how to study the community so that the needs of students can become central to the teaching-learning process — courses or experiences in studying the community may be required to help students at the college level acquire the skill. For example, the teacher in the inner city will probably need to know how to build a satisfactory self-image in students, how to work with parents who may have a dislike for education, and how to cope with children with special problems, such as those from poor or single-parent homes.

Universities and colleges can meet many of these needs with only minor changes in their current teacher-training programs. The instruction of students, for example, should include a method of helping prospective teachers understand the need for a commitment to the community. This might include an early exposure to teaching in a community setting through laboratory sessions in actual classrooms or practice teaching experience as early as the freshman year.

A greater understanding of, and commitment to, the community could also be promoted through the on-campus courses prospective teachers take. Courses focusing on studying the community, building community-based curricula, and learning about community action models are some of those that could be offered.

The extended student teaching experience near the conclusion of the training program could also be utilized to help prospective teachers understand the dynamics of the community. For example, a recent graduate from Iowa State University taught in a high school for half a term as the first portion of her student teaching assignment. She then worked in an inner city community action program where she was involved in youth and adult programs. The Nebraska Opportunities for Volunteers in Action (NOVA) program is also being utilized by some future teachers as a a method of intensive involvement in community programs. Participants spend an entire year planning and implementing community programs.

The Service Function

An important service function for the university initiating an increased emphasis on the community will be the in-service education of teachers already on the job. This might be an alternative to teachers going back to college for graduate training or it might include some arrangement for graduate credit to be applied for programs and courses off the college campus. The focus of these in-service programs will not only be updating on methods and information but also the provision of information and approaches for a greater community involvement and understanding.

The service component of a community-oriented university will also involve working in communities on special problems. For example, university professors from a school of education could help schools to establish a community school program. Another example would be members of a university psychology department helping a community to establish a mental health or community crisis clinic.

Another service that universities could perform is the teacher training of instructors that work in technical schools, community colleges, or private trade schools. These instructors have often had little or no formal training on how to work with adults; personnel from schools of education could provide teacher-training opportunities at these institutions.

The Research Function

There are many community problems, such as school dropouts, the unemployed, and the under-educated, that require solutions. Unfortunately, we know little about how to solve them. Universities could fulfill a great need by concentrating some of their efforts and resources toward action research on specific community problems such as those described above.

Another important research need is the evaluation of ongoing community educational and other types of programs. Institutions of higher education could carry out the total evaluation of various community projects and programs or could at least provide evaluation consultation.

The development and field-testing of new teaching methods and techniques is a third research function that could benefit the educational efforts of communities. Public schools and universities could cooperate on determining where new methods were most needed and various schools in the communities might serve as testing grounds for refinements of the methods.

NEW FUNCTIONS TO CONSIDER

There are various new functions related to the community that universities and colleges could assume if commitments were made and if supporting resources were granted. One new function might be educational planning. This could include a closer cooperation with state departments of education, increased planning and consultative support to regional resource centers or service units, and the provision of a centralized computer data bank of educational information.

The educational planning function could expand to helping local school districts in such areas as proposal-writing to qualify for federal programs, instituting more systematic programs of accounting or record-keeping, and helping schools make long-range projections on community educational needs. Universities might even employ planning specialists that work with a variety of public and private agencies in planning their educational programs. The educational investment scheme proposed in Chapter 7 could be the framework utilized by such specialists for decision-making.

Universities throughout the country might make an increased commitment to dealing with urban schools and their problems. Assistance here could include such functions as training community-change specialists to work in urban environments, training community leaders regardless of their educational backgrounds, and helping to establish better patterns of communication and cooperation among citizens, school officials, and leaders in urban communities.

Another function might be the training of more teachers skilled at working with adults. These specially trained teachers could work in adult basic education programs, adult high schools, and public school adult education programs. Perhaps some universities could institute undergraduate programs specifically designed to prepare educators of adults to meet this need.

DEVELOPING NEW COMMUNITY THEORY

A suggestion was made in the first chapter that a modern theory for studying and understanding the community was needed. Hopefully, the information presented in the preceding chapters has helped to build some basic foundations for this theory.

It is suggested further, that universities should take the lead in developing a theory and corresponding knowledge base that can be used to help communities solve their many problems. Leadership at the community level will be enhanced by leadership at the university level. Education can be used to solve community and societal problems, but it must be as a process that shows people how to help themselves. The goal of higher education has always been to help individuals grow in knowledge and ability. Let's extend that goal to the community.

SELECTED BIBLIOGRAPHY

Books

BERDAHL, ROBERT O. *Statewide Coordination of Higher Education*. Washington, D.C.: American Council on Education, 1971. 285 pages. Bibliography. The author conducted a study to determine the many changes that have occurred in higher education during the past ten years. Such topics as planning, budgeting, programs, and problems are discussed. The reader will gain some understanding of the changes required if higher education is to be more successful in solving various problems.

BOSLEY, HOWARD E. *Teacher Education in Transition*. Volume I, An Experiment in Change; Volume II, Emerging Roles and Responsibilities. Baltimore, Maryland: Multi-State Teacher Education Project, 1969. 345 and 365 pages, respectively. Appendix. These volumes describe the activities of a multi-state teacher education project designed to improve teacher education. Case studies of various state programs were included. The volumes discuss the use of teacher aides, the use of media, and new and needed developments in teacher education.

KNOWLES, MALCOLM S. *The Modern Practice of Adult Education*. New York: Association Press, 1970. 384 pages. Index. Appendixes. This book describes the emerging role and technology of adult education. The author also presents and describes his conceptualization of a new approach to teaching, especially the teaching of adults. He distinguishes between "pedagogy," the teaching of children, and "andragogy," the helping of adults in their learning pursuits. The book has wide application to the training of teachers for community education.

Periodicals

Current Issues in Higher Education. Formerly an annual publication of the Association for Higher Education, National Education Association; currently, it is not being published. Back issues of the journal contain many articles related to higher education and teacher training.

The Journal of Teacher Education. Published quarterly by the National Commission on Teacher Education and Professional Standards, National Education Association, Washington, D.C. The journal contains various articles related to teacher education.

Films

Andragogy—Video tape—30 minutes—black and white. This video film is a discussion about a new concept in adult education by Dr. Malcolm Knowles, Boston University, and Dr. Roger Hiemstra, University of Nebraska. The information has application for teacher training. The tape may be rented through the Nebraska Educational Television Council for Higher Education, University of Nebraska, Lincoln, Nebraska.